The Pleasure
of
Your Company

The Pleasure
of
Your Company

Entertaining Friends...
and Enjoying It

Elinor Guggenheimer

ILLUSTRATED BY
ROLLIN McGRAIL

CLARKSON POTTER/PUBLISHERS
NEW YORK

Published by Clarkson N. Potter, Inc., distributed by Crown
Publishers, Inc., 201 East 50th Street, New York, New York 10022

CLARKSON N. POTTER, POTTER and colophon are
trademarks of Clarkson N. Potter, Inc.

Manufactured in the U.S.A.

Library of Congress Cataloging-in-Publication Data
Guggenheimer, Elinor C., 1912–
The pleasure of your company : entertaining friends and enjoying
it / by Elinor Guggenheimer. — 1st ed.
1. Entertaining. I. Title.
TX731.G78   1990
641'.4—dc20   89-29024
ISBN 0-517-57472-1

10 9 8 7 6 5 4 3 2 1

First Edition

To Randy, with gratitude for the times he has helped me to find my mislaid date book; for patience and perspective when I predict an imminent disaster; and, most of all, for filling our lives with laughter.

Contents

The Pleasure
of
Your Company

Overture

A very special toast
To every very special host
From sea to sea across the fruited plain
To those who have the gift
Of giving all of us a lift
Who are entertaining when they entertain
To canapés and dips
That really shouldn't pass our lips
To Beaujolais Nouveau that we have sipped
To friends whom we have made
And to the weekends we have stayed
In guest rooms that were perfectly equipped
To every special date
When we can meet and celebrate,
To friends who ask us out and foot the bill
To time that goes too fast
To parties of the past
And parties that we hope to go to still.
It's all enormous fun
Like an island in the sun
A garden in an interlude of leisure
So, darling, take my hand
Let's go listen to the band
And drink to friendly company, and pleasure.

A very long time ago, Randy, my patient and persevering husband, and I moved into our first apartment. Until then we had lived in a rented hotel flat, waiting until our savings reached a level that made a real home feasible. (Admittedly, "real homes" cost very little to rent in 1933 and were abundantly available.) So on the first of October, the date on which all New Yorkers moved, in the years before scarce housing and rent control turned us into permanent house plants, we rescued our wedding gifts from my mother's storage closet; and by four o'clock that afternoon we had unpacked the six silver cocktail shakers, the lamp made of some kind of animal skin, which was the gift of a distant cousin, and the rest of the essential paraphernalia that would enable us to keep house.

Two months later, with a new baby in the second bedroom and diapers boiling all day on the stove, we were faced with the prospect of having our first guests in our as-yet-untried dining room. The guest list was limited to my widowed mother, my grandmother, Randy's parents, and his sister. I can still recall the sick feeling with which I anticipated the "pleasure" of their company. There were several small mishaps that evening, which I thought of at the time as catastrophic, but our guests were enchanted. I learned later their expectations had been so low that they were rather easily impressed. But when I think back across the years I no longer recall the nature of the mishaps. Instead I remember a sudden swelling of pride, looking to the head of the table where my young husband sat, and feeling that we were very adult and very much in control.

Since then we have given literally hundreds of receptions, dinners, children's parties, and buffets. I cannot imagine what our home, or our lives, would have been like if we had not shared them often with our family and friends. Certainly not as rich, or as happy! I still do have a tendency to worry, or at the least to become a little anxious, while planning a party and while waiting for guests to arrive. Anxiety is partly an inheritance from my mother (a constant victim of pre-party perturbation), but it is more the result of caring, and wanting everything to be just right for our guests. Still, over the years practice has lessened the worry, and today concern is almost completely overshadowed by a pleasurable sense of anticipation. It is this feeling that I want to share with those of you who for one reason or another are reluctant to entertain guests or who actually go through the processes of entertaining with some of the same enjoyment you may reserve for visits to the dentist.

A party should not represent the terminal point in an obstacle course; nor should anxieties grow to such proportions that they become barriers. By learning to deal with any unrealistic fear rationally, it becomes possible to develop a relaxed attitude, while at the same time recognizing that there is a serious purpose to entertaining. Parties can fulfill a vital community function, providing opportunities for making friends and enhancing business relationships; I have always believed that more important deals are conceived, and helped through gestation, at parties than in corporate boardrooms.

Besides the positive aspects for the gross national product and the economic health of the floral, food, music, and service industries that depend on social events, families are held together by birthday and other holiday celebrations. The fabric of a society is formed by the weaving process that takes place at the formal dinner, the cocktail party, and the backyard barbecue.

Hospitality is an important aspect of life, one treated with reverence in tribal huts, in caves, and in castles. The regard in which the laws of hospitality have been held is evident in the fact that a host even in a primitive society was constrained to assure the safety of sworn enemies at his table. On a less historical or philosophical note, it is clear that giving and going to parties is fun. The human animal today, existing in a world of ecological and political uncertainty, needs as many opportunities for fun as possible.

In a long lifetime of taking pleasure in the company of friends in our home we have had our share of problems. Each one has served as a lesson and has given me the confidence to continue entertaining as well as to offer advice, which I actually attempt (not always successfully) to follow myself. I've found that the small amount of effort that may be needed to overcome reluctance and to reach out to friends whom you want to see is more than amply compensated by a full and busy life.

1

Phoolish Phobias

How to Handle the Fear of Entertaining

My life's begun to bore me
For my erstwhile friends ignore me
Just because I'm scared to have them in my house.
They're saying that I slight them
And it's true I don't invite them
For I'm not a social lion. I'm a mouse.

My parents gave dinners for eight or more guests several times a month, and sneaking into the kitchen to pilfer snacks or watching through a crack in the dining-room swinging door was as beguiling to me as Nintendo is to the present generation of children. The atmosphere at these dinners was always stiff and structured. Mother considered buffet suppers suitable only for clambakes on a beach, and she equated civilization with the number of forks, knives, and spoons necessary for the consumption of the many courses served at her table. In a world where there were no frozen or convenience foods, her menus were remarkably elaborate. As impressive as the food and service were, however, I suspect the parties were never much fun. I do know that Mother would have considered the entire evening a failure if a waitress were to remove a plate from the wrong side.

When I married it was taken for granted by my new husband, Randy, and by our parents that we would continue the tradition of entertaining in our home, and in the formal manner they considered appropriate. But from the beginning we rejected the rigid rituals, partly because they were so complicated and partly because we never found them enjoyable.

It takes time to develop confidence, and I approached entertaining with a good many phobias: Something was sure to go wrong; no one would really want to come; I didn't have the right equipment; the hot food would be cold, and vice versa. Nevertheless I persisted, probably because the importance of entertaining had been ingrained in me during childhood. Gradually I learned to enjoy having company, and I hope and believe that our friends have enjoyed being our guests over the years.

For those who are reluctant to give parties or merely to have guests in their homes, I can offer assurance that fears *can* be overcome. Besides, they are usually based on illogical assumptions about the difficulties involved, the potential for failure, and the amount of work that is necessary. It does not require a doctoral degree to give a party, nor is there any mystique connected with entertaining. A little familiarity with the process is easy to acquire and serves to overcome any number of underlying phobias, including the most basic:

Phobia 1: The "I Don't Know How" Syndrome

Entertaining is easier for people who were raised in a household where company was a constant fact of life. For others, such details as making a guest list, issuing invitations, selecting a menu, and arranging seating may seem overwhelming. Some of our friends sidestep problems by entertaining in restaurants. Having parties at home requires more effort than leaving all the arrangements to a maitre d' or manager, but restaurants lack the informality and warmth of sharing one's home with friends. Still, many people are willing to spend a great deal more to entertain in rented premises because they overestimate the difficulties and remain unaware of the plusses of entertaining at home.

The first party, like any first plunge, is the hardest. Even those of us who grew up in households where parties were held frequently may have to go through a learning process when we are suddenly on our own. One long-ago bride who is now an accomplished cook recalls phoning her fishmonger in a panic, insisting that he had sent her green shrimp instead of the pink shrimp her mother always served. There was a pronounced sigh at the other end of the phone, followed by the patient assurance that, "If you just put them into boiling water for a minute, I promise they will look just like Mother's shrimp."

Knowing how to prepare various dishes, and how much of what to serve, is really a matter of swimming in uncharted seas and learning where the shoals and reefs may be. No matter how many parties you have observed through a crack in the door, everything will still seem unfamiliar on the first few tries. The quantities may be wrong or the wine may not be as chilled as it should be or the table may not be perfectly set. Each of these miscalculations represents a step or stroke to impeccable hostdom. And there are ways to avoid some of these problems even during a learning phase: Consult others who have had more experience; ask the butcher at the supermarket and the wine merchant at the liquor store about quantities; and by all means err on the side of abundance. Avoid lamb chops, squabs, or other individual items, so that the last guest to be served will not find the platter bare because of a miscount or because a humorist among the guests took two. (We had such a guest at a dinner, and we handled the situation by laughing delightedly, and asking him kindly to replace the second squab on the platter.) If you are determined to serve nonflexible food such as squabs or chops, order several extra in case there are unexpected guests. Freezers were designed for the hostess who miscalculates on the plus side. And each party simply increases the accuracy of the planning process.

Fortunately it takes very little time or practice to move from paddling in the shallow end to swimming the distance. Assuming that reluctance to entertain stems from lack of experience, and with no family tradition to consult for guidance, there are three ways to learn: copy your friends, start getting experience, and read this book.

Phobia 2: The "Something Will Go Wrong" Syndrome

For some people, the conviction that something is bound to go badly inevitably becomes a self-fulfilling prophecy. Fortunately, experience teaches that what hosts consider to be calamities are usually no more than amusing incidents as far as guests are concerned, to be quickly forgotten or merely the subject of an affectionate anecdote in the future.

It is patently impossible to guarantee perfection at any party, but I can assure hosts that guests rarely notice imperfections. From time to time even the most experienced hosts have encountered what they might consider disasters. The guest of honor reneges at the last moment; the tried-and-true recipe collapses; the caterer hired two months in advance fails to appear; or two of the most carefully selected guests decide to disagree, not calmly but with the kind of passion that leads to pistols at dawn. I recall one rather unfortunate evening when I brought together two adversaries in a takeover situation; another when I placed a guest next to her ex-husband's lawyer; and still another when guests who should have enjoyed meeting sat silently with apparently nothing in common to discuss. In each case some extra effort on our part improved the atmosphere, although sometimes the effort required was considerable.

Mishaps and mistakes rarely make more than a passing impression on guests. No one at a dinner (except possibly the hostess) will notice if the glassware doesn't match or if one of the plates is chipped. On one embarrassing occasion our housekeeper decided, without my knowledge, to change the menu and serve asparagus as a first course, later with the main course as a vegetable, and, still later, chopped into the salad. As the asparagus kept reappearing to my dismay, the only comment was from one guest who said, appreciatively, "I just love asparagus!"

Nor should you allow last-minute cancellations or additions to a guest list to disturb you. They are unlikely to affect your guests unless you let them know that you are upset. On one January evening some time ago when we had planned a large party, an unexpected blizzard hit the city at the last minute. It was too late to reset the table and, besides, we kept hoping that more guests would make it through the storm. When we went in to dinner, Randy and I and the two couples who had arrived sat at one end, looking down at the long stretch of wine glasses, service plates, and silverware. The six of us were served by a hired butler and two waitresses. With so much attention, and so much extra wine being poured, the evening ended on a high note, although it may have been the ridiculous Edwardian setting that turned us into giggling adolescents.

Over the years a number of less dramatic occurrences have made parties unexpectedly colorful. I recall one dinner during which I emptied a plateful of ice cream on my lap when a guest wondered whether our dessert plates were Spode, and I hastened to satisfy her curiosity by turning my plate over to inspect the marking. And I am unlikely to forget the Superbowl party at which the bartender "improved" the Bloody Marys by adding cream to the mix. The guests tried them and voted to do without Bloody Marys. We improvised with whatever we were able to find in our larder: some fruit juice and vodka, Cokes with rum, and soft drinks. Fortunately the game was exciting and the party was fun.

I am convinced that any situation is salvageable if the hosts remain unflappable. In other words, mishaps have little effect on guests or the success of a party, and worrying that "something may go wrong" as an excuse for avoiding parties in one's home is a very poor excuse indeed.

Phobia 3: The "Nobody Loves Me" Syndrome

Even the most assured among us from time to time wonders if anyone really loves us. There are moments when almost everyone identifies with the lyric, "Nobody loves me, everybody hates me, I'm going in the garden and eat worms." That condition is particularly liable to occur when you sit down with paper and pencil ready to draw up a guest list. If the condition is unfortunately chronic, you may never get beyond the point of staring at a blank piece of paper. Suddenly you have few if any friends, and you become convinced that anyone you might decide to invite will certainly refuse.

Worms are unappetizing, and the best cure for such depressing thoughts is immediately to invite those whom in a better frame of mind you consider friends. Their enthusiastic response is sure to provide a healthy dose of ego enhancement. People are always pleased to be invited to a party. In fact, when I hear about invitations my friends have received, even from acquaintances I barely know, I feel a quite irrational qualm at not having received an invitation myself.

It is heartwarming to know that your presence is desired. Besides, everyone from the busy executive to the equally busy housewife, or house-husband, appreciates a break from cooking dinner or eating out in restaurants. An invitation to a friend's home provides a welcome change, and one for which people truly are grateful.

Normal people (and in spite of occasional flights of eccentricity, most people fall within a normal range) will be delighted to accept your invitation, will look forward to the event, and will even make an effort to "sing for their supper." If your invitations are issued in sufficient time to avoid conflicts with other events, it is safe to assume that most of those you invite will ultimately make an appearance, and in a party mood.

Phobia 4: The Home Sweet Home Syndrome

Some people may have an exaggerated nesting instinct that interferes with their willingness to share their homes. Home is an intensely personal place, and having strangers, even friendly ones, scrutinize the sacrosanct premises is almost like being caught in a state of partial, or total, undress. The fear of adverse criticism, of allowing others to assess our home, our possessions, and our taste in furnishings is a cause of anxiety with which I am personally familiar.

I am no longer paranoid about my nest, but there are still times when the cold and critical eye of an outsider seems, if not terrifying, at least inimical. Suddenly nothing is quite right. The paint is peeling in one corner of the dining room. There are cracks in the living-room wall that I had secretly hoped would disappear. I refrain from assuring my guests that, of course, we intend to have the entire apartment painted, and we're just waiting for the summer. (Several summers have already come and gone, and we dread the summer when we decide that we can no longer wait.)

Before a recent dinner party several of our dining-room chairs developed arthritis and were sent for rest and rehabilitation to a neighborhood carpentry shop. They were replaced at a dinner by assorted bridge chairs. At about the same time I noticed several unfortunate worn spots in the hall carpet. Also I had been aware for a while that the bedspread in our room should have been donated to a thrift shop. Nonetheless, the party went on as planned. Through years of practice I have learned to ignore cosmetic shortcomings on the nights when we have guests, just as I have managed to ignore them during the guestless nights of the year. And of course I know better than to call attention to imperfections.

Sometimes in the past when we had guests who were richer or more chic than we, or who owned estates that had been manicured recently by interior and exterior designers, I worried about what they would think of our home, and of us. I now realize that I am denigrating my friends if I believe they will like us less because of a crack in the paint, or that they will even notice it unless I call it to their attention. Besides, most of them have one or two plague spots in their own homes, no matter how impressive.

As far as the worn bedspreads are concerned, guests heading for the bathroom at a late hour after dinner are more liable to notice beds longingly than critically. This does not mean, of course, that you will not want to put the best possible shine on your home. Pride in the appearance of the nest is one indication of the value you set on your guests. But if fear of entertaining is based on insecurity about the elegance of your possessions, you are attributing to friends a snobbishness that is probably only a reflection of your own.

Phobia 5: The "It Will All Slip Away from Me" Syndrome

For many people, feeling in control of an event gives them self-confidence. Yet some potential hosts perceive parties as essentially beyond their control. You may suffer from a premonition that guests will refuse to participate in the entertainment that has been so carefully planned. You fear guests may sit waiting fretfully for dinner to be ready and make no effort to talk, then become recalcitrant and refuse to follow you to the dining room once dinner is announced. None of the conversations will conform to the pattern you had devised; nor will the guest of honor talk to the lady on his right, although you invited her for the express purpose of amusing him.

Most of such fears are ephemeral. Probably none of these events will ever come to pass, although there are times during the party, when everything is going according to schedule, that hosts may suddenly feel that they are not in control. A successful party does take on a life of its own, and actually this can relieve an insecure host of responsibility.

If you suffer from the rather ordinary anxieties associated with responsibility, you can learn to relax. There are very few situations in which more control can be exercised than by the host at a party. Of course, "control" requires that the desires of guests be considered and that the host be flexible enough to adjust to those desires. But ultimately *you* are in complete command of the guest list, what the guests will eat and drink, and even at what time they may politely retreat. Everything from seating arrangements to timing is decided by you, the host. And proof of the power you exert is that guests are always flattered to be chosen to sit next to you.

The feeling that I might lose control of an event means to me that I have allowed my personal insecurity to dominate my thinking. I have invented a problem that doesn't exist. A few deep breaths and an assumption of the appearance of confidence, even if it is a pose, bring events back into focus.

Phobia 6: The Solo-Flight Syndrome

Planning and giving a party with the cooperation and assistance of someone else should be a happy experience, but if you live alone there may be genuine reasons to be anxious about entertaining. When there seems to be no one with whom to discuss plans or to help serve drinks or to keep the guests amused while you're putting the finishing touches on dinner, the feeling of isolation can be painful. And yet it is even more important for the single person to entertain friends, to keep an active social life, and to fight loneliness than it is for couples.

I have been lucky. When we have company I depend on Randy to back me up, to keep the conversational ball in the air, and to flirt with the retiring female guests. But for a number of our single friends, entertaining without the support of a co-host seems overwhelming. The recent loss of a spouse by death or divorce especially can leave a person feeling stranded, although this may not affect men as adversely as it does women. Despite all the efforts at liberation, single men are in greater demand than single women, and the latter must make more of an effort to fend off isolation, retain friends, and expand their worlds.

Fortunately no one has to swim alone. Two or three potential hosts can join together, inviting mutual friends or even each other's friends, and share the costs and responsibilities. Progressive parties with one course at each of several homes, or parties where everyone brings one course to the home of the host, lighten the burdens for the single person. And if the party *is* a solo flight, rather than a group effort, there will surely be one or more guests who can be recruited as auxiliary hosts and even as bartenders; or one special friend who can be designated as a co-host, to help keep the party moving while the host is moving the dishes.

If you cannot recruit an auxiliary host from among friends, you may turn to relatives for help. Think twice, however, before enlisting your mother or sister. Their ideas of entertaining may clash with yours, and they will be unlikely to refrain from expressing their differences.

Phobia 7: The Food, Glorious Food Syndrome

Edible complexes prevent some people from entertaining. Food is, after all, the centerpiece of a party. It is not unrealistic, therefore, to be concerned about what to serve and how to serve it. And yet the mere act of presenting a delectable salad of warm quail with fresh chervil does not establish you as a host *extraordinaire*, although a sloppily prepared and tasteless meal may carry a message that the host is unconcerned about the company's pleasure. In fact, esoteric cuisine has very little to do with a good party, and if your friends are the nonadventurous type, or prone to allergies, exquisite food can have an adverse aftereffect. A mundane or prosaic menu may actually be more appealing under certain circumstances.

We had such circumstances a few years ago. We were living in the suburbs at the time, well before the age of cholesterol, and we had invited twenty-four guests for a gourmet dinner. The menu, as I recall, included a marvelous warm lobster course, squabs, baby vegetables, and chocolate soufflé. At four in the afternoon a violent thunderstorm knocked out all electricity in the entire area, leaving our cooking equipment in a state of impotence. At ten o'clock that night, when it became clear the kitchen would remain out of commission, Randy finally co-opted an assistant from among the guests and drove to a nearby deli. We feasted on ham and cheese sandwiches, while twenty-six squabs, neatly prepared for roasting, went to bed in a freezer after the power was restored at midnight. Everyone called the next day to tell us it had been a great party, even in a squabless state.

If the anticipated rare roast emerges from the oven in a shade of unappetizing puce, if the ice-cream cake comes out of the freezer too hard for even an ax to penetrate, if almost everything about the menu is wrong, the party can still be right. For every dish to be a disaster is as rare as the roast should have been, and hardly worth contemplating. Besides, with the growing interest in calorie counts, the Pritikin diet, and Weight Watchers, friends may be grateful for a reason to resist a dish or two.

Planning a menu has been made simple by the plethora of cookbooks, food magazines, and the weekly newspaper columns offering recipes. If these fail to provide inspiration, there are friends to be consulted, or other people's menus that you may have enjoyed at a recent party, which you can plagiarize. And of course the proliferation of takeout establishments and caterers has made it relatively painless to decide what to serve. But whether the meal is to be prepared at home or by a caterer, it is a good idea to pay some attention to contrasts in consistency, flavor, and color. Obviously no one would serve rice accompanied by mashed potatoes on one platter, but I do recall a dinner at which the hosts served breast of turkey in a white sauce with white rice and cauliflower. It looked rather bland assembled on one plate.

Aside from taste and balance, you may be concerned that your menu have eye appeal. This too should not become a major problem. Bunches of herbs, watercress, sliced radishes, and carrots, even edible flowers can dress up a platter, and it is not difficult to arrange food so that it looks appetizing. No one expects the home cook to produce ice sculptures.

If possible, in planning a meal it is considerate to observe the partialities and allergies of particular guests, but this is a thoughtful touch that most guests do not expect, and certainly it should not worry you if your memory fails. And if your kitchen and talents cannot produce French cuisine, you might recall that Eleanor Roosevelt served hot dogs to the king and queen of England when they visited her home at Hyde Park. I understand that they enjoyed the meal thoroughly.

If even a carefully planned menu produces a hot soup that is cold and a cold dessert that is unexpectedly warm, as long as the hosts remain cool, the reaction of the guests will be accordingly both warm and forgiving.

Phobia 8: The Undefined Discomfiture Syndrome

Some of the same factors that contribute to the "Something Will Go Wrong" Syndrome are present in the general malaise that afflicts the sufferers of the Undefined Discomfiture Syndrome. Those who feel that entertaining is too much work, that they will never have the time to handle it all, or that they are not capable of organizing and remembering every detail often invent excuses or imagine problems. They may create situations based on remote possibilities as reasons for avoiding decisions and facing imagined failure. They ask themselves questions such as: Will the guest of honor have to enter through the kitchen because the front elevator is broken? Will the caterer fail to appear or be hours late? Will we run out of ice, vodka, or wine? Will I forget to invite my mother-in-law, or, even worse, will she come and embarrass me? Will the wine have turned to vinegar? How will I know what kind of wine to serve with the meat? Will I remember to buy place cards? And if I don't have room for all my friends, will some of them be insulted?

This kind of generalized malaise accounts for some of the reasons why people defer entertaining. If each time before or during a party you suffer from misgivings, you will certainly hesitate before staging a repeat performance. But there are a number of ways to cope with this. If you cannot overcome the worries by facing them squarely one at a time, by handling those that can be overcome by literally forcing yourself to complete a guest list, order the ice, and taste the wine, you might ask a friend who entertains successfully to act as your party planner. Or, if you can afford the cost, hire a professional planner who will take over all aspects of the party. On the day, or the night, of the event keep very busy. Before the party you can spend time rechecking details. If you have checked and cross-checked so that there is nothing more to be done, you may have to resort to watching television, reading a book, or writing an overdue letter. If none of this works, you can always try to concentrate on problems greater than yours, such as what might happen if there is an earthquake or what we should do about the elephants in Kenya. And if that too fails, I believe in trying laughter—even if it is at yourself.

Laughter has been called the best medicine, and it is useful in almost any situation, especially when there are others in the house such as a spouse or companion or a hired helper to talk to and to laugh with. If you're worried that the roast has been in the oven too long waiting for the arrival of an overdue guest, take everyone's mind off it with a joke, an anecdote someone else has told you, a funny episode that you witnessed or that involved your child or even the delivery man who brought the groceries. Keep it short, and if you can't think of anything funny to say, keep smiling anyway. Guests do not expect you to be a professional humorist, just a friend in good humor. And humor is a better sauce for an overcooked roast than a perfect *glace de viande.*

It is not easy in every case to identify the reasons for discomfiture. Reluctant hosts may be suffering from fear of the effort involved in entertaining, a kind of psychological inertia (although I have been told by a psychiatrist that this particular malady is undocumented in any reliable medical journals). Or childhood traumas may have resulted in a general feeling of inadequacy. In neither case is the expense of therapy warranted. The cure is still in this, as in other cases, learning by doing.

If you have never worried about having company, or if you have overcome previous malaise, you are fortunate. If not, and if any of these phobias describes your problem, there is a cure. Go to the phone immediately and invite three or four friends to your home for brunch, lunch, tea, or supper—or for whatever you choose. You will never know how much fun it is to have company unless you begin. What starts as travail becomes apple pie after one or two efforts. You will find yourself saying, and meaning it, "How lovely to see you! You look marvelous! Come in and make our home your own!"

Of course you may not phrase your welcoming speech that way, but that doesn't matter if what is conveyed is a feeling of hospitality. And once you have succeeded in making your guests feel comfortably at home, you will not only feel comfortable yourself, you will find yourself planning the next event even before the last guest has departed.

2

The Cast of Characters

Drawing Up a Guest List

Here is my list and I'm ready to use it
It's liable to change since I'm liable to lose it.
The mix will be perfect; the numbers just right,
For here are the guests whom I plan to invite:

Margaret Truman;
Simon and Newman;
Susan and Nan;
And an unattached man;
Milton and Carol;
Trumps by the barrel;
Mathilda and Mario;
Friends here from Paree—oh;
Calvin and Kelly;
And Liza Minnelli;
Senators, two or perhaps even three,
Oh what a glorious night it will be!

uest lists need not be dotted with impressive names to project a good party. There are, in fact, very few rules that apply to the preparation of a guest list, and none that are immutable. Before the first phases of planning and implementing a party I always intend to review date books, so that I will be reminded of those people whose parties we have attended, and to whom we are therefore indebted. I try, also, to think of people whom we enjoyed seeing at these parties and whom we would like to see again. Finally, in making up the list I consider whether those I am inviting will enjoy being together. These intentions are admirable, and if carried to their conclusions should result in a foolproof guest list. The problem is that even if I do draw up such a list I tend to invite people I run into casually, rather than those whom I have so carefully planned to ask. Oddly enough, the party that results from bringing together an irrational assortment seems to work, which leads me to believe that the orderly choice of guests may be, in the end, rather unimportant.

It is wise, however, to plan the guest list with an eye to the future seating plan—to give some thought to what disparate guests may find in common to discuss and to be prepared for the eventuality that a certain number of the invitees may not accept. On the other hand, it is fun to bring together people who may not know each other well, if at all, and who therefore may make an effort to be agreeable. I do try to invite guests who will be pleased to meet or to see each other, or who will be flattered to have been included in such a charming group. But since I am a left-of-center Democrat married to a right-of-center Republican, dinners at our home are inevitably a mishmash, which creates a certain amount of lively disharmony ab initio.

Apples and Oranges

My mother, who generally avoided advising me on many of the more serious aspects of life, was prolific with suggestions on social procedures. She believed that it was imperative to invite to any one affair only those people who were recognizably compatible. This translated into putting doctors with other doctors, Wall Street tycoons with

response; a senator is always a celebrity and therefore socially acceptable even to members of the opposition party.

I knew that I was breaking all the rules about creating a harmoni-
ous mix of people. The party was to include Gustave Levy, chairman
of the Wall Street firm of Goldman Sachs; Brooke Astor, New York's
most charming civic leader and philanthropist; Mildred Hilson,
prominent socially and a personal friend of all Republican presidents;
and Irving Mitchell Felt, then-chairman of Madison Square Garden
and a real-estate enterpriser who was active in politics and cultural
affairs. To the list we added leaders of the Democratic and Liberal
parties and a sprinkling of potential large contributors.

To accommodate everyone we placed tables in several rooms, each
seating ten or eleven people. During dinner Bobby moved from table
to table so that each guest had a chance for informal communication. After dinner we cleared the living room and, with most of the
guests sitting on the floor, Bobby stood in front of the fireplace,
answering questions and sharing his dream for our state and for the
world.

For me the evening had a magical quality. There were fifty-four
guests altogether and, as intended, it was dominated by Bobby
Kennedy. I always thought of him as a shy man who seemed a little
out of place in the world of politics, as though his role had been
forced on him and never completely accepted. Still, he carried great
conviction when he spoke, and he cared deeply about injustice, about
those who suffered from it, and about children. Everyone in the room
that night was caught up by his message.

The party worked, perhaps because of the guest of honor or because there was a purpose or theme or maybe just because intelligent
conversation is always a potent ingredient in a mixture that makes
a successful event.

Once you've narrowed down your guest list to what you hope will
a convivial crew, it is essential to review that list with an eye to
number and space. A party should never be so overcrowded that
guests are reminded of rush hour on a subway or of a tropical heat
wave. The other side of that proposition is the empty-auditorium
effect. Undercrowding is as destructive to enjoyment as its reverse,
the chilling effect of a half-empty room, or of a dance floor where

bankers, and committed members of the Republican party with all
of the above. By her standards, if Democrats were to be invited they
would be happy only with stage personalities, social workers, and
liberated women. The underlying concept was to ensure that everyone at a party would be, as nearly as possible, a mirror image of
everyone else, or at least so similar in appearance and life style as to
guarantee perfect harmony.

I have discovered that perfect harmony may not produce a perfect
party. A group of my childhood girl friends who meet mother's
criteria of compatibility, who share an interest in bridge, exercise
classes, and gossip, and who have at times even shared an interest in
each other's husbands, make no effort to be convivial when they are
together at parties, and the result is boredom for all involved. As
much as any group could be they are homogenous (or, in this case,
femogenous), but inviting them for dinner followed by bridge has
proven to be anything but felicitous. In fact, the introduction of a
few outsiders with different ideas and lives seems to make rather dull
mirror images suddenly sparkle. The reverse of this, however, and an
almost sure guarantee of failure, is inviting one outsider into an
intimate group where he or she will be forced to stand with a fixed
smile listening to the other guests discuss people and events that are
totally unfamiliar. As a lecturer, I have been the miserable guest of
honor at a reception where there seemed no way to break into the
animated exchanges about local affairs and characters. A good mix
of guests requires enough diversity to make everyone feel equally
involved.

An exception to the caution against total homogeneity are parties
for members of the society groups featured in newspaper columns,
who may prefer being invited with each other. And of course there
are special occasions, such as birthdays and holidays, which are limited to family and close friends. The theme of such events makes
homogeneity appropriate and takes care of the boredom factor.

There have been evenings when we have had guests who appear
to have only combativeness in common, and at such times I have
wished that I had adhered to homogeneity in preparing the guest list.
When the atmosphere becomes troubled it is up to the hosts to pour
oil, not on the fire, but on the troubled waters. A light anecdote, a

toast, any interruption may work. Still, even at the risk of introducing people with firmly held opposite views, I am convinced that a certain amount of mishing and mashing is wise.

Count Your Clunkers

My conviction about the positive value of mixing people is probably a convenient excuse for the fact that I have never been really well organized and for my inclination to issue enthusiastic invitations to friends whom I run into on the street. As a result I always say to Randy on the day before a party, "This is going to be a nightmare. This is the worst I've ever done. You see, if the Auchinclosses had been able to come, or the Tisches, or Muriel Siebert—and I had planned on one of them at least—they could have acted as the glue, but even then it wouldn't have gone at all—and you absolutely have to help me with the seating"—which he doesn't! Randy, when facing a party that I am describing as a potential shipwreck, is apt to race for the lifeboats, leaving me to drown; or ask with irritating logic, "Why did you ask this particular bunch in the first place?"

I do have an answer to that. Most of us are required at times to invite guests who would hardly qualify under the heading of "charming." They may be disagreeable relatives, ex-schoolmates who have not developed since graduation, or business acquaintances we need to cultivate but who are unlikely to charm anyone. These are the people I classify as "clunkers." They tend to sit passively looking morose and, worst of all, consulting their wristwatches at periodic intervals. If the party is working well they may be swept along; if they remain resistant, at least they are apt to go home early.

On any scale of desirable party people, clunkers register near zero. At the upper end, near ten, are the "uppies." These are the guests who sing for their supper. They can be counted on to keep a party going, and if they are true "tens," they are not only good conversationalists but superb listeners. In developing a guest list it is wise to avoid a preponderance of clunkers. I would suggest that the ratio of clunkers to uppies not exceed one to four.

V.I.P.s

It helps, too, to have one or more stars, or special guests v rest of the party will perceive as being important, particul; esting, glamorous, or knowledgeable in an esoteric field they are prepared to be fascinating. If the field has somet! with entertainment or sex, so much the better, since th universal interest. A guest of honor immediately elevates a the ordinary to the extraordinary. It also enables you to i! tional fascinating guests with whom you have only a i quaintance but who may be a friend of the honoree; or ar acquaintance whom you know slightly but who may have in meeting the honoree. Honorees do not have to be though it's pleasant and exciting if they are. If, howeve unknown, it is easier to elaborate on their curricula vitae are in the public eye. (The extent of the elaboration at depends on my mood, and even more on whether R preoccupied to undermine my efforts at hyperbole.)

One of the most eclectic guest lists I've ever prepared of the most carefully assembled. Many years ago I gave Bobby and Ethel Kennedy while he was serving as the U senator from New York. I had been working with him opment of small parks and on the special project that Bedford-Stuyvesant in Brooklyn. Because he had not York before winning election as our junior senator, he fe people of influence and with important ideas whom he an opportunity to meet and who should have access many people in the "establishment," without ever ha him or even having met him, viewed him with a good d

I don't remember whether it was his idea or mine, in the winter of 1966 we drew up a list that includec Republicans, Wall Street tycoons, Vietnam doves wh President Kennedy's escalation of hostilities in South personal friends of every political coloration. We re ances from one hundred percent of those invited. It curiosity or the lure of a celebrity that elicited such an bankers, and committed members of the Republican party with all of the above. By her standards, if Democrats were to be invited they would be happy only with stage personalities, social workers, and liberated women. The underlying concept was to ensure that everyone at a party would be, as nearly as possible, a mirror image of everyone else, or at least so similar in appearance and life style as to guarantee perfect harmony.

I have discovered that perfect harmony may not produce a perfect party. A group of my childhood girl friends who meet mother's criteria of compatibility, who share an interest in bridge, exercise classes, and gossip, and who have at times even shared an interest in each other's husbands, make no effort to be convivial when they are together at parties, and the result is boredom for all involved. As much as any group could be they are homogenous (or, in this case, femogenous), but inviting them for dinner followed by bridge has proven to be anything but felicitous. In fact, the introduction of a few outsiders with different ideas and lives seems to make rather dull mirror images suddenly sparkle. The reverse of this, however, and an almost sure guarantee of failure, is inviting one outsider into an intimate group where he or she will be forced to stand with a fixed smile listening to the other guests discuss people and events that are totally unfamiliar. As a lecturer, I have been the miserable guest of honor at a reception where there seemed no way to break into the animated exchanges about local affairs and characters. A good mix of guests requires enough diversity to make everyone feel equally involved.

An exception to the caution against total homogeneity are parties for members of the society groups featured in newspaper columns, who may prefer being invited with each other. And of course there are special occasions, such as birthdays and holidays, which are limited to family and close friends. The theme of such events makes homogeneity appropriate and takes care of the boredom factor.

There have been evenings when we have had guests who appear to have only combativeness in common, and at such times I have wished that I had adhered to homogeneity in preparing the guest list. When the atmosphere becomes troubled it is up to the hosts to pour oil, not on the fire, but on the troubled waters. A light anecdote, a toast, any interruption may work. Still, even at the risk of introducing people with firmly held opposite views, I am convinced that a certain amount of mishing and mashing is wise.

Count Your Clunkers

My conviction about the positive value of mixing people is probably a convenient excuse for the fact that I have never been really well organized and for my inclination to issue enthusiastic invitations to friends whom I run into on the street. As a result I always say to Randy on the day before a party, "This is going to be a nightmare. This is the worst I've ever done. You see, if the Auchinclosses had been able to come, or the Tisches, or Muriel Siebert—and I had planned on one of them at least—they could have acted as the glue, but even then it wouldn't have gone at all—and you absolutely have to help me with the seating"—which he doesn't! Randy, when facing a party that I am describing as a potential shipwreck, is apt to race for the lifeboats, leaving me to drown; or ask with irritating logic, "Why did you ask this particular bunch in the first place?"

I do have an answer to that. Most of us are required at times to invite guests who would hardly qualify under the heading of "charming." They may be disagreeable relatives, ex-schoolmates who have not developed since graduation, or business acquaintances we need to cultivate but who are unlikely to charm anyone. These are the people I classify as "clunkers." They tend to sit passively looking morose and, worst of all, consulting their wristwatches at periodic intervals. If the party is working well they may be swept along; if they remain resistant, at least they are apt to go home early.

On any scale of desirable party people, clunkers register near zero. At the upper end, near ten, are the "uppies." These are the guests who sing for their supper. They can be counted on to keep a party going, and if they are true "tens," they are not only good conversationalists but superb listeners. In developing a guest list it is wise to avoid a preponderance of clunkers. I would suggest that the ratio of clunkers to uppies not exceed one to four.

V.I.P.s

It helps, too, to have one or more stars, or special guests whom the rest of the party will perceive as being important, particularly interesting, glamorous, or knowledgeable in an esoteric field on which they are prepared to be fascinating. If the field has something to do with entertainment or sex, so much the better, since these are of universal interest. A guest of honor immediately elevates a party from the ordinary to the extraordinary. It also enables you to invite additional fascinating guests with whom you have only a passing acquaintance but who may be a friend of the honoree; or an attractive acquaintance whom you know slightly but who may have an interest in meeting the honoree. Honorees do not have to be famous, although it's pleasant and exciting if they are. If, however, they are unknown, it is easier to elaborate on their curricula vitae than if they are in the public eye. (The extent of the elaboration at our parties depends on my mood, and even more on whether Randy is too preoccupied to undermine my efforts at hyperbole.)

One of the most eclectic guest lists I've ever prepared was also one of the most carefully assembled. Many years ago I gave a dinner for Bobby and Ethel Kennedy while he was serving as the United States senator from New York. I had been working with him on the development of small parks and on the special project that he started in Bedford-Stuyvesant in Brooklyn. Because he had not lived in New York before winning election as our junior senator, he felt there were people of influence and with important ideas whom he had not had an opportunity to meet and who should have access to him. Also, many people in the "establishment," without ever having talked to him or even having met him, viewed him with a good deal of animus.

I don't remember whether it was his idea or mine, but sometime in the winter of 1966 we drew up a list that included conservative Republicans, Wall Street tycoons, Vietnam doves who had opposed President Kennedy's escalation of hostilities in Southeast Asia, and personal friends of every political coloration. We received acceptances from one hundred percent of those invited. It may have been curiosity or the lure of a celebrity that elicited such an overwhelming

response; a senator is always a celebrity and therefore socially acceptable even to members of the opposition party.

I knew that I was breaking all the rules about creating a harmoni-
ous mix of people. The party was to include Gustave Levy, chairman
of the Wall Street firm of Goldman Sachs; Brooke Astor, New York's
most charming civic leader and philanthropist; Mildred Hilson,
prominent socially and a personal friend of all Republican presidents;
and Irving Mitchell Felt, then-chairman of Madison Square Garden
and a real-estate enterpriser who was active in politics and cultural
affairs. To the list we added leaders of the Democratic and Liberal
parties and a sprinkling of potential large contributors.

To accommodate everyone we placed tables in several rooms, each
seating ten or eleven people. During dinner Bobby moved from table
to table so that each guest had a chance for informal communication. After dinner we cleared the living room and, with most of the
guests sitting on the floor, Bobby stood in front of the fireplace,
answering questions and sharing his dream for our state and for the
world.

For me the evening had a magical quality. There were fifty-four
guests altogether and, as intended, it was dominated by Bobby
Kennedy. I always thought of him as a shy man who seemed a little
out of place in the world of politics, as though his role had been
forced on him and never completely accepted. Still, he carried great
conviction when he spoke, and he cared deeply about injustice, about
those who suffered from it, and about children. Everyone in the room
that night was caught up by his message.

The party worked, perhaps because of the guest of honor or because there was a purpose or theme or maybe just because intelligent
conversation is always a potent ingredient in a mixture that makes
a successful event.

Once you've narrowed down your guest list to what you hope will
be a convivial crew, it is essential to review that list with an eye to
number and space. A party should never be so overcrowded that
guests are reminded of rush hour on a subway or of a tropical heat
wave. The other side of that proposition is the empty-auditorium
effect. Undercrowding is as destructive to enjoyment as its reverse,
and the chilling effect of a half-empty room, or of a dance floor where

one can really swing one's partner, is not conducive to the feeling of intimacy essential in a party of any size.

The following are the guidelines that should be used in reviewing a guest list before the invitations are mailed:

1.   **If at all possible, do not include known adversaries.** If your sister-in-law and your husband's favorite cousin really dislike each other, plan two family gatherings rather than risking a thoroughly unpleasant evening, unless the event is so large that they will have no trouble avoiding each other. Of course this applies equally to divorced couples. If it is absolutely necessary to include both ex-es, even if the new spouses are comfortable with each other, be sure to enlarge the party so that mutual avoidance is possible.

2.   **Depending on the purpose of the party, try to invite people who do not see each other regularly, or who may never have met but whom you believe will enjoy each other.** Deciding who will enjoy an evening with whom is subjective. If you find two of your friends to be fascinating, it is fairly safe to assume that they will like each other as well. If their points of view on any known subject, particularly politics, are strong and opposite, I suggest caution, no matter how attractive you find both of them.

3.   **Include a "star," if possible.** The honored guest need not be a celebrity. At a family gathering grandfather may be the honored one, or a granddaughter who is about to leave for college may be featured as the star. At a formal dinner of people who are strangers to each other, having a guest whose achievements one can describe in a toast is apt to make guests feel they have been invited to a very special party, and one that will enable them to gloat a little when describing the event to friends who were not there.

4.   **Make sure that the majority of your guests are the type who enjoy parties, who are flattered to have been invited, and who will make an effort to help everyone have a good time.** Clunkers should be dispersed over several parties and never concentrated at

one event. If you are tempted to finish them all off at one time, remember they will probably not be grateful for a dull evening. You will have gone to expense and effort without pleasing anyone, not even yourself.

5.   Invite the right number for the available space. Guests should be able to move around comfortably, but rattling around in empty space is liable to make guests uncomfortable.

6.   Try to like everyone of your guests at least a little bit and show at least as much enthusiasm as you feel. You may have to become an actor for a few hours, even with members of the family with whom you have had less than cordial relations. Since everyone reacts well to being liked, you will probably find your opinion of a guest changing as a result of your convincing performance.

3

Spreading the Word

Preparing and Issuing Invitations

The invitation looks sublime
I hope that it arrives in time
But that depends on Uncle Sam
Who frankly doesn't give a damn

I ssuing invitations should be a pleasant task, just as the anticipated party will be a pleasure. Whether the potential guests are
notified by phone or by mail, the message should promise a
happy event. The tone of voice or the appearance of the envelope and its contents should be agreeable, and formal invitations
should suggest an aura of elegance. But whatever shape the invitation
takes, it is most likely to elicit the desired response if it simply seems
inviting.

I have a virtually foolproof method of handling invitations, both
those I receive and those I issue. After responding to those I receive,
I enter the information in my date book and put the actual invitation
in a tickler file. When we are the inviters I prepare a dated list of
those I plan to invite; put a check mark next to each name as I send
an invitation or make a phone call; add a second check when I receive
an affirmative response; cross off the names of those who respond
negatively; and dispose of the list on the day after the party. At least
those are my intentions. A method is only as perfect as its implementation, and mine suffers from chronic deviation.

One instance in particular illustrates the lapses in my record keeping rather vividly. It was a few weeks before Christmas and I had
planned a rather large party to celebrate the holidays. Unexpectedly
my doctor decided it was a good moment (for him!) to take care of
a minor surgical problem. I protested, but the doctor and Randy
won, and so I took off for the hospital, leaving my Christmas shopping and my desk in disarray. Fortunately, or so I thought, an accom-
modating friend agreed to notify the guests I had expected for dinner
that week. I gave her my list and relaxed. Sometime later she reported with a good deal of bitterness that she had conscientiously
called everyone on the list, and that all of them, in turn, gave her
the impression that she had lost her mind. Having thanked her
politely, they said in mystified tones, "But I was never invited."

I am still not sure where the list came from and why it was lying
on my desk. Unfortunately for the efficacy of the system, I have not
overcome my habit of keeping odd pieces of paper that should have
been relegated to the trash basket and, even worse, of inviting friends
I happen to meet in the supermarket. In the latter case I do try to
remember and to enter their names on my list as soon as I get home.

Telemarketing

To avoid some of the possibility of errors occurring, I usually issue my invitations by phone. The phone makes it possible to receive an immediate response and to revise the guest list accordingly, as I can check off or delete names as I go. If one guest is unable to come, I can substitute another. The success of this method of issuing invitations depends, of course, on being able to reach people at their homes or offices on a first or second call. Otherwise you may find yourself involved with the lengthy and boring process of communication between answering machines.

Phone-answering machines seem to be a necessary evil of our busy time. We are enmeshed in technology, which was intended to simplify life, but actually often results in confusion and a good deal of wasted time. When I phone someone to issue an invitation and find myself in touch with an answering machine, I often prefer to hang up and resort to the mail. This might not be the case if people would give more thought to the type of message they record. There are friends I avoid calling merely because I find listening to their taped voices almost unbearable. For instance, I dread the sepulchral tones of one of my friends whose machine demands the time and the date in addition to a brief message. Having to remember the time and date is so unnerving that I am usually unable to speak when I hear the beep.

A worse alternative is the pseudo-humorous message: "Hi! This is Mary. I mean this is Mary's answering machine not Mary because Mary herself doesn't happen to be here, but you can leave your message—after the beep of course—with my dear G.E. machine, which takes messages better than I do anyway—and it's nice of you to call and do leave a message in iambic pentameter or any other way you want, only we won't promise to listen for more than five minutes. Have a happy." Messages of this type have one advantage. After hearing the same recorded frivolity each time I call, I may decide to cross Mary off the list and invite someone else.

The same caution should apply to the issuer of the invitation. When you leave messages on other's machines, they may be forced to respond to your machine. You owe consideration to those whom you have asked to call, and that means keeping your recorded messages as brief as possible.

If the line isn't constantly busy so that you spend an hour trying to reach someone you wish to invite, and if the answering machine is not doing the answering, a phone call has the advantage of making an invitation seem warm and personal, providing that the caller has cultivated a pleasant voice. A flat, monotonous voice evokes the image of a flat, monotonous party. If you have any question about the way you sound, test yourself with a tape recorder. You may find that your voice needs lowering, softening, slowing, cadencing, or that it needs clarity. A pleasant voice has influence, a fact that has been underestimated by our educational systems.

There is an additional reason why an invitation issued personally is desirable: It enables guests to ask questions if they choose, or if you have omitted details. They may even ask who else will be coming, which might appear rude or overly inquisitive but does help guests determine what to wear. It is quite legitimate, however, to withhold the information if you choose.

Once upon a time I was terrified of phoning anyone I didn't know quite well. On one occasion that I still recall vividly, I had to call the wife of one of the senior partners in Randy's firm to invite her and her husband for dinner. (The firm was considering a young man for partnership, and apparently the social graces of the young man's wife had to be inspected.) The senior partner's wife was under orders from her husband to accept, and she showed exquisite skill in conveying the idea that an evening with Randy and me was not a choice she made freely. Our conversation on the phone was as frigid as was the subsequent evening, and even though the invitation was accepted I experienced a painful feeling of rejection. Fortunately, disagreeable people are scarce, and disagreeable responses to invitations are very infrequent.

Through practice, my phone skills as well as my confidence have improved. I can now dial an acquaintance and say, "Hello, Mrs. Overman? This is Elly Guggenheimer. I hope you remember that we met three weeks ago at Selma's. We both enjoyed meeting you and your husband and particularly discovering that we have so many mutual friends. I said I would call you, so here I am. I hope you're free next Tuesday night. We're having a cookout and we would love to have you join us. Six-thirty, very casual, and at our house."

In spite of obstacles, such as occasional chilly responses or long-winded answering machines, telephoning invitations remains my first choice.

Put It in Writing

If the party is to be large, phoning may be impractical, and even if the affair is to be quite small, there are times when it is more efficient to write rather than to attempt to reach people by phone. In the latter case, a note on personal stationery is appropriate. The language may range from polite formality to the coffee-in-the-kitchen variety, depending on the type of event and the level of familiarity with the recipient. It should convey a sense of the size and the type of the event so that guests are prepared: "Dear Mrs. Outerman, John and I hope you and Mr. Outerman will join us for dinner with the Innermans on Saturday, February 30, at 7:30. There will be just six of us, and dress is informal. Please call me at 555–1212 and let me know if you can be with us. Sincerely, Helen Upperman." This conveys the necessary information, as does: "Joy dear, We're having a bash. Well, not exactly a bash—we have some out-of-towners and I need you and Ace to impress them. There will be ten or twelve if everyone can come. Seven o'clock, Saturday the thirtieth—Okay? Call me!"

Of course, neither of the above may be you, and since a letter is a way of putting your personality on paper, it should reflect your style. In a sense it should also resemble a press release that announces an event, describing the product (a dinner, a brunch, a reception) and providing the information on where and when. It should also indicate the size of the gathering and provide accurate information on dress, so that one couple does not arrive in blue jeans when everyone else is in evening clothes. And if your home is off the beaten track, a map should complete the invitation. Guests who have spent hours searching for your home are unlikely to arrive in a party mood.

Randy and I came rather close to terminating a normally happy marriage on one wintry night in Scarsdale. We had been given directions—inadequate ones, as it turned out—and for half an hour we had been touring dark and unfamiliar areas, becoming steadily more confused and more furious with each other. We finally spotted our destination, although it was not at all where the directions had led us to believe. The house was well lit and a large number of cars were parked in the driveway and on the road.

Once inside, we were pleased to discover several people we knew and very pleased to be offered drinks and quite delicious hors d'oeuvres. Our hostess was absent, but we assumed she was busy in the kitchen or talking to guests in another room. What we failed to discover until we had been there for half an hour was that we were happily eating and drinking at a party in the home of complete strangers.

The Creative Touch

In addition to any necessary factual information, your invitation should also convey the flavor of the event. It is good to remember that most of us receive such large quantities of unsolicited mail, and are so continually bombarded by words, that in a sense we are competing with public-relations and advertising experts every time we write a letter, communicate by telephone, or send an invitation. If only the bare essentials are included, the invitation may actually resemble a subpoena, evoking a less-than-happy response.

Actually, we recently *did* receive a subpoena as an invitation to a party. Cute!—which is not to be confused with "creative" or "original." "Cute" should be used with the greatest of caution, and only when "clever" is impossible. In this instance the invitation ranked as clever and appropriate rather than cute because the party was in honor of a distinguished jurist.

A few years ago I resorted to a cute invitation for a party, and it helped make the party successful, thereby proving again that there are exceptions to every rule. I had told a friend, in a burst of affectionate enthusiasm, that I would dearly love to host a cocktail party–

buffet in honor of her fiftieth birthday. She promptly and with no demur accepted the proposition, embraced me, and expressed her great gratitude. I felt a little less enthusiastic when I received her list: sixty of her dearest and closest friends, not one of whom could be omitted. I was working at the time in a government office near New York City Hall, and a crisis erupted shortly after I had received the list, putting the whole event completely out of my mind. Three weeks before the scheduled party, and with the crisis still erupting at work, I woke up. No invitations had been sent, or written, or even purchased. Making phone calls to such a large group was out of the question. I had only business stationery in my office and the stores in the city hall district were not the type that carried social stationery. Recognizing my desperation, one store manager agreed to search his shelves and found four dusty boxes of baby-shower invitations.

The invitations were appallingly cute. With no other choice available, however, I made the best of what I thought at the time was a bad situation, and in due course sixty people received invitations to a baby shower for a fifty-year-old matron, with the added instructions to bring an original nursery rhyme and an appropriate gift for less than a dollar. Taking advantage of my inadvertent theme, I bought baby decorations, children's games, and a special birthday cake.

To my surprise, the party was a huge success. Even though the invitations were late in arriving, people broke dates because the party sounded so "special." A baby shower for a fifty-year-old was "adorable," or so I was told at intervals during the party. If I had sent a conventional invitation it would never have conveyed such an impression of special thought, nor would I have conceived of the theme. Although it is usual for a theme to antedate the selection of an invitation, there are times when an invitation can inspire the theme, food, decorations, and even the guest list.

Unless the event is formal, in which case you have less creative freedom, an unusual or attractive invitation will enhance anticipation. This can mean spending considerable time searching through racks in a store or, better still, creating your own invitation with the help of a computer and word processor. It is not necessary to be particularly talented or creative. Kindergarten-level artistic ability often works very well. Of course, having someone in the family who does have talent can be a help. I am blessed with a daughter-in-law who is extremely creative, and I call on her for ideas. A little while ago she and I spent several hours developing a theme for her husband's birthday, and several more working on the details of the invitation. Based on the response of the guests, and the pleasure of the birthday boy, both efforts were worthwhile. Since golf is the overwhelming passion in my son's life, the theme was golf and the invitation was a reproduction of a golf scorecard, with our country club seal. The inside had the requisite information plus the picture of a swinging golfer and an inquisitive Canadian goose. The printer who works for a company with which I am connected helped us with the design.

At a party on our fiftieth anniversary, given by our children, the cover of the invitation featured a photograph of Randy and me taken half a century earlier on the weekend before our wedding. In the picture we are standing with our arms around each other. Although I don't recall that anything seemed risible to either of us on that nerve-wracking weekend, it is a happy picture and it gave the invitation a happy feeling. The words on the cover were, quite simply, "Fifty years and still laughing."

We have received, and sent, many different kinds of invitations: a circus poster for (you guessed it) a circus party, a scene with cutout animals for a safari party, a toy boat with an invitation attached to a sail for a boating party, and a front-page facsimile of a newspaper for an anniversary party. Elaborate invitations may require expensive professional help, but for those of us whose resources are more limited, a neighborhood printer who will be handling the job is usually glad to offer advice, to supply graphics, and to help with the format and type for an invitation.

Formals

A formal invitation is the easiest, since it requires—in fact, allows—very little originality. Raised letters, or engraving, on white or ivory stock of good quality are obligatory. Like any invitation, it forecasts the type of party it will be; the message is formal and elegant. Often the name of a special honoree appears above that of the hosts. Formal invitations are usually appropriate for dinners, receptions, weddings, large balls, and in some instances formal lunches in honor of special guests or events.

The words "formal" and "formula" derive from the same Latin base, and therefore formal events, as well as invitations, are shaped by formulae. Invitations conform to the following "formulae," with small variations:

In honor of
Senator and Mrs. Richard Roe

Mr. and Mrs. John Doe
request the pleasure of your company
at dinner, 7:45 P.M. The Manor House
1075 Locust Avenue
Formal   *RSVP 555-1212*

In most cities, potential guests for formal events require a substantial amount of advance notice. For an ordinary dinner party, when I want to ensure a certain mix of guests, I allow four to six weeks. For events like weddings, it was once considered proper to send invitations three weeks ahead of the day. Air-travel problems have changed all that. We now have friends in many parts of the world, who must be given time to make reservations and to arrange to be away from home or office for more than just a day. When our friends John and Frances Loeb planned a dance to celebrate an important anniversary, their friends received notice almost four months in advance; and I suspect that invitations went to desirable single men even earlier.

A formal, or informal, invitation today usually includes a return card and envelope. At one time this would have been considered insulting, since it would have carried the implication that the recipient was so ignorant of proper manners that he or she wouldn't know enough to respond promptly. Customs have changed. The return card is quite proper now.

Listing a phone number after the letters RSVP may work just as well, since more and more people seem to find even the return of a stamped card too difficult. Perhaps the easiest, although by no means the most reliable, system is indicating "regrets only" on the invitation. If a precise count is needed, follow-up phone calls will have to be made.

A reminder card is a kind of insurance policy—just in case one or more of the expected guests are the type who keep less than accurate date books or if your invitation was delivered rather casually or in case there was an error on the invitation. A friend once sent us an invitation with the wrong date. Fortunately, a reminder card prompted me to call for clarification. Without such a card I would have missed the party, and both my hostess and I would have been unhappy.

A reminder card should be in the same type as the invitation, and the details that were on the initial invitation should be repeated:

REMINDER

Mr. and Mrs. Randolph Guggenheimer [or, in less formal circumstances, Elly and Randy] expect you for dinner at our home on Saturday, February 30, 7:30 P.M., black tie.

(For an informal event a postcard containing the relevant information is all that is necessary as a reminder.)

Finally, before you mail the invitation or the reminder, take a good look at the envelope. For very special events, such as weddings, a calligrapher is worth the price. For other occasions, since my penmanship has never developed beyond second grade, I sometimes find a friend endowed with good handwriting skills to help. I never type the address on an invitation. It might be mistaken for an ad or an appeal for funds and be discarded unopened. And I never use a cheap-looking envelope. Even if I open such a letter, I feel that the party will be as tacky and uncared-about as the envelope.

Errors caused by keeping inaccurate lists, failing to give accurate information, or failing to indicate that the party is formal and requires evening dress are not world-shattering. When my friend who kindly volunteered to notify guests that my party was cancelled reported her failures to Randy, he found the right list and managed to reach everyone who had really been invited. When my chagrined hostess in Scarsdale, who was waiting to serve dinner, received our call from the home where we had landed, she gave us improved instructions and called our inadvertent hostess the next day. The two became friends.

And at a formal dinner when a guest arrived in mufti, we made him feel so welcome that he was convinced all the others were incorrectly dressed. Since then, however, we have made sure to scrutinize invitations we send by mail, or to take extra time and pay extra attention to the information we provide when we invite people by phone. Surprise parties are for special occasions, and it is not considerate to surprise guests whom there is no reason to surprise.

4

Variations on a Theme

Selecting and Implementing Party Motifs

"Come and join our trip to China!"
"Come and eat at Looey's diner!"
Any theme a bit unusu-al
Any theme that will amuse you all
Any idea you can dream
Can become a party theme.

A theme can be as elaborate as a costume ball designed to re-create the court of Marie Antoinette or as simple as a birthday party with posters or pictures that describe the life of the honoree. If a party is being given for a defined purpose other than the purely social one of having friends for lunch or dinner, there is an implicit theme. The degree to which the theme is embroidered depends on the hosts.

Parties that are given for a special purpose and, therefore, have a built-in theme include bridal showers and stag parties, birthday and anniversary parties, tributes to someone who has just won a Pulitzer prize or its equivalent, and going-away events for world travelers. Having a purpose or theme for a party makes the event special, and it is easier for guests to feel in the mood to have fun when a party is special.

A theme can transport a party from a parochial setting to outer space; or from small town to international glamour. Most of us live our lives in small towns even if we live in big cities, and we welcome the chance to move into a wider world, if only for one evening at a neighbor's house.

New York is a city of small towns, and many of our friends who have traveled to exotic places like Borneo have never visited the other towns that are part of their own city; or if they have, it is as American tourists. That means they have had little or no communication with the members of the other communities that comprise the mosaic called New York.

There is a large Chinese population in lower Manhattan, living in what is referred to as Chinatown. At various times, friends of ours have gone to restaurants in Chinatown and have inevitably been served Americanized versions of food from menus in English. In the period before President Nixon opened the gates, China and its varied customs had become increasingly remote, and so we decided it was time to do some exploration. Although Peking and Shanghai were closed to us, Pell and Mott streets were not, and so we called some Chinese friends and asked them to help us plan a "trip to China."

Our friends organized a twelve-course banquet in a restaurant in Chinatown, and none of the food was familiar fare. In addition, they acted as our tour guides, providing information about the customs and history of their community, a brief verbal tour of mainland China, and a fascinating short film of current-day Shanghai, which Americans had been unable to see in more than twenty years. As a theme it was a little unusual but lots of fun. Ethnic restaurants in many cities may be the destination of "trips to foreign ports."

Even the thoroughly American deli or diner can be used for an unusual party, although the food will not be as exotic or the theme as educational. One proprietor of a diner (his establishment did happen to be a franchise operation, but he was marvelously cooperative) rented his entire premises to friends of ours for a brunch party. Our friends had been entertained recently by an important, or self-important, gentleman at The '21' Club in New York. They decided to reciprocate in equally elegant style. Before the event they had coached the maitre d' (a short-order cook) on greeting the guests with the appropriate hauteur and making a great show of seating them in the "right part of the diner." The guest of honor took a while to recognize that he was being feted in a somewhat proletarian version of '21.' (The pancakes were delicious!)

Having a purpose or a theme for a party can actually make planning easier, since it may predetermine the type of invitations, decorations, food, and entertainment; and at the party itself it gives guests who have trouble starting conversations an immediate topic to discuss. Themes set a framework and unify an event. They may require originality and a fair amount of work to implement, but with so many features of the party determined in advance, the host ultimately has fewer decisions to make.

Costume Parties

Costume parties leave most of the decisions to the guests, who are expected to arrive looking beautiful, funny, and surprisingly original. They are almost always fun, because costume parties are akin to improvisational theater, in that they enable the withdrawn and the inhibited to become free spirits and to express themselves.

Costumes provide both the decoration and the entertainment at a party, thereby relieving you, the host, of two areas of concern, but it is a important to know your cast of characters. Guests are not always cooperative. Most of our male friends are willing to appear in tuxedos if their wives tell them they have no choice, but they may rebel at having to impersonate Louis XVI. Faced with the need to wear anything other than clothes from his regular wardrobe, Randy is apt to develop a sudden touch of the flu. Hosts need to take into consideration the resistance a female guest may encounter in persuading her husband that an authentic Louis XVI has to wear a powdered wig, or that a clown has to have a bright red nose.

Large costume balls, which were common during the 1920s, are now just memories, but they were wonderful at the time. I remember a costume party for a twenty-first birthday. One group of guests, dressed as camels, shieks, and slave girls, stopped traffic as they crossed the street to the hotel. Others went in outfits rented from well-known theatrical establishments, or in costumes created specifically for the party. It was all a long time ago in an era when parties were almost as expensive as the parties for tycoons today, except that then the parties were for the young and marriageable, rather than for the elderly and remarried.

Parties with Personality

Less expensive than a costume party and just as much fun was a recent party given for the birthday of a lady who is in the business of providing art for corporations. The theme, not surprisingly, was art. Pictures of the honoree obtained from her mother included one of her husband with their children (Dada-ism); one of her about-to-be daughter-in-law (new acquisitions); one of her entire family (permanent collection); and one taken when she was four months old (neoclassicism). Each guest was asked to bring a "masterpiece" costing less than fifteen dollars as a gift. Except for one extraordinary bit of pornography, most of them were not memorable, but the process of opening the various gifts was hilarious.

Over the years we have used a variety of themes for events celebrating a variety of occasions, or in celebration of nothing. One that I recall fondly was a "Trip Abroad" that several of us gave to console some friends who had canceled their trip abroad that summer because a recession had sent a few shock waves through Wall Street. We procured blank airline tickets and filled them in with the names of friends who had been invited to meet at "the airport" (our apartment) for takeoff. After the check-in procedures, which included the distribution of itineraries and a short travel lecture, we boarded the plane (a rented bus). During our "flight," a steward and stewardess (roles assigned to willing friends) offered pre-prepared Bloody Marys and peanuts.

We touched down first at the Brooklyn Museum, where we had arranged to have a guide take us on a docented tour. Most Manhattan residents almost never go to Brooklyn, and yet the museum is quite marvelous, with one of the world's greatest collections of ancient Mediterranean art, as well as authentic period rooms that would induce tourists in Europe to go many miles out of their way. The visit was a treat.

We continued sight-seeing in Brooklyn until we reached Coney Island, where we had arranged for "lunch at Maxim's by the sea" (Nathan's hot-dog emporium). Everyone was given an envelope with sufficient "foreign currency" (two dollars American) for lunch and one ride in the amusement park.

Our trip abroad may not have compensated entirely for the real thing, but it was a great party, and it's still remembered with pleasure by our traveling companions.

We had another kind of theme party recently. Our guest of honor was Dr. Ruth Westheimer, the very well known sex-therapist, and because her reputation preceded her the theme was obvious. Part of the implementation was carried out through the table decorations. Some years before we had visited Nepal, where we were bemused by the open, uncritical, and accepting attitudes toward sex. While there, we bought seven small bronze statuettes of groups numbering two, three, four, and even five collaborators in activities requiring great dexterity. The figures were arranged around a floral centerpiece, to the consternation of our housekeeper, Lucy. Dr. Ruth registered delighted amazement rather than shock and, in due course, such admiring enthusiasm that by the end of the evening we were delighted to give her one of the small figures.

I suppose if we had taken our theme somewhat further we might have asked our guests to come in nightgowns and pajamas, but I do recognize that there should be a limitation on the length to which themes are carried.

On yet another theme, a few years ago I gave a Caribbean party for guests who had been left behind in the frozen north when large numbers of their friends had escaped to the tropics. Our guests were instructed to dress in outfits suitable for Nassau or Barbados. It happened to snow that night, and I have always wondered what the taxi drivers who delivered the guests to our house would have thought of the shorts and bathing suits under the furs and woolens. As it was, straw hats, white shoes, and tennis rackets must have looked odd to them.

For this excursion to the tropics we labeled each table with the name of an island, and we gave each guest a hotel brochure that identified their "resort." The decorations consisted of cardboard palm trees that I had created (each of which I labeled as such, in case they were unrecognizable). We served planter's punch; we played calypso music on tapes; and we invited everyone to do the limbo, which most of our guests managed to do quite well by stepping *over* the rope. The party was a huge success, possibly due to the planter's punch.

We have used all kinds of travel themes, particularly when someone has just returned from, or is planning a trip to, an exotic place. In each case we focused on the theme with travel posters, itineraries, and passport pictures taken by Polaroid. In exchange for highlighting their trip, we exact a pledge from the traveling guests to refrain from sharing their memories or their photographs with us.

Travel parties have included Japanese and Chinese parties for friends who are about to depart for the Orient; Greek parties with an expert to help with Greek dances for travelers to Athens and Corfu; and a round-the-world party for a friend who had written a travel book. Book parties for some of our literary friends provide a simple theme: namely, the book. We use pictures of the author and blowups of the book cover as decorations. The number of volumes sold as a result has rarely compensated for the time and trouble, but the gratitude of the authors and publishers does.

Birthday Parties

One of the most obvious themes is a birthday celebration. Birthday parties may or may not include the presentation of gifts, but there are two traditions that I believe must be observed: the birthday cake and the atonal singing of "Happy Birthday to You." The cake has whatever number of candles are appropriate, except in cases where a very large number of years are being celebrated. My children settle for one large candle on my birthday, since the correct number carries an inflammatory risk.

You can, however, get more elaborate. A few friends took over a popular disco recently to give a birthday party for Betty Friedan. Some of us staged a musical version of Betty's life and work, which we rehearsed for weeks, and with a good deal of temperament on the part of the lyricists and the actors. Since it was a large party, we had to avoid living-room amateurism, or so we hoped. The costumes were funny, the songs were apropos, and the show itself was, alas, still a recognizably amateur production. Nevertheless, the guest of honor was pleased and the audience was sympathetic.

Someone asked me recently which of all the theme parties I had given or attended was the most memorable, and I immediately thought of a party for a gentleman friend who was celebrating his sixty-fifth birthday. We had always teased him about his interest in ladies; he rather fancied himself a Don Juan, although I suspect he has been a loyal husband who enjoys looking but would be terrified of touching. We decided to give him the perfect party, which meant providing him with a full-fledged and somewhat déclassé harem. Ten of us arrived in skintight black satin, purchased from a bargain basement in lower Manhattan. We wore long red and blonde wigs, long artificial eyelashes, and a great deal of makeup. Since none of us had frequented bordellos, we may have lacked authenticity, but the guest of honor and we, his harem, were all quite pleased with the results. The entertainment, if it can be characterized as such, consisted of amateur belly dances, which were undoubtedly ridiculous, but good friends are tolerant, and grateful for effort. The party was, well, memorable.

When, or if, we give a party that is a little unconventional, I am aware that the mood of the guests will play a significant part in its success or failure. If they are not in the mood to be silly, or to join in the spirit of our creative undertaking (and I admit that Randy avoids aiding or abetting any efforts that are too original), I might find myself alone, dancing in the middle of the room while our guests eye me suspiciously. Clearly a host cannot force guests to participate. If even one of them decides that I am being absurd, the weight of the wet blanket may be too heavy to lift. On the other hand, ninety-nine percent of my friends are the type who want to enjoy themselves and are not only willing to go to some lengths to be good sports but are grateful for the opportunity. The other one percent won't come back, but then we probably won't invite them.

It is perfectly reasonable to give parties without a story line, and for *no* reason. But if there is something to be celebrated, and if therefore the party has a motif, there is an almost implicit guarantee that the evening, or the day, will be exceptional and enjoyed by the guests.

5

Who's Cooking?

Amateurs versus Pros

I enjoy being waitress and cook. That's because
My guests will reward me with cheers and applause
But there's nothing more likely to lighten my mood
Than when someone else is preparing the food.

P arties do not produce themselves. If you are a moderately good cook, and if you can stay calm while arranging the service and eventual cleanup, you may not require outside help. For those who prefer to concentrate on the guests or who arrive home from the office ten minutes before the doorbell is expected to ring, assistance and assistants are obtainable, and without too much effort.

Do It Yourself

I like to cook, and when I want to avoid the vagaries of professional cooks, butlers, and other help, and when our housekeeper is not there, I find the do-it-yourself method both feasible and fun. Until World War II, however, I was an abysmal cook with no understanding of the chemistry of food. I followed recipes (simple ones) slavishly and was astonished when the flour and butter thickened a sauce, and equally astonished when the hollandaise turned into scrambled eggs. During World War II, with almost no available housing near the airfield where Randy was first stationed, we shared a house with five other desperate couples. It was agreed that the wives would take turns preparing supper for the whole group. On my night to act as cook, the lumps in the gravy were described by the others as new and deadly weapons. I was permanently barred from further contact with the preparation of food and assigned to house-cleaning tasks for the duration.

Today I consider that I am an excellent cook, although I rarely attempt to prepare and serve a meal for more than eight at a time without some help. I have tried once or twice to manage twelve guests on my own (except for Randy), but I found that being the cook and waitress gave me no time to enjoy my guests, and vice versa. There are books and articles by the score to which I refer, designed to instruct me on how to sit, cool and collected, chatting with guests as though the dinner was cooking itself. I admit, however, that I have yet to discover any menus that don't require last-minute ministrations. I know that making a list of everything that has to be done, and then doing it in advance, is helpful. The rolls should be in the oven ready for the last warm-up, the butter in the fridge on a proper plate for service, and the wine breathing on the kitchen table. But even a menu that consists of a one-dish casserole, a salad, and a prebaked pie needs watching, stirring, and carrying. If I can leave the living room quietly—and if my not-always-cooperative husband doesn't stop the conversation by asking, "Where are you going?"—preparations can be inconspicuous. The less hubbub, the more relaxed are the guests.

If I were better organized, I might invite guests to join me in the kitchen and to observe the last-minute activities, which can be fun for the observers and companionable for the cook. I have never been that courageous, and certainly I have never dared to serve dinner in the kitchen, although that would have advantages, such as eliminating the need to carry the food to another room. Unfortunately, we have neither a pass-through nor the necessary counter space, nor do I trust my friends, let alone my family, to stay out of the way and resist giving advice.

When I *am* in the do-it-yourself mode I have one cardinal rule: I never accept a volunteer. Occasionally I have recruited a friend or family member, but even that is rare. Dinner can be significantly delayed if I have to stop twenty times to answer, "Where is the coffee pot? What do I put the rolls in? Where are the little forks? Are you using salad plates?" and so forth. It is difficult to proceed when a helpful volunteer blocks the refrigerator every time I want to open it or drops a glass on the floor because "My hands were slippery. Where do you keep paper towels?" In the case of one well-intentioned gentleman, who cut his finger at the very moment when he was holding forth about his prowess at carving, we had to leave our guests and spend the evening in a hospital emergency room.

In the past I have enlisted the help of my spouse and my children (who required a stipend). There was never a question of recruiting my mother or mother-in-law, but if either had been willing, I would have refused. Both of them were ladies with strong opinions, and only one commander-in-chief is practical in a kitchen.

A small backyard or patio affair with a portable grill can be handled *en famille,* and it is a good answer to the proposition that those who can't take the heat should get out of the kitchen. Randy, who is terrified of kitchens, will happily don a ridiculous apron and inhale charcoal fumes by the hour. The rules applying to volunteer help in a kitchen do not apply on the patio, and enthusiastic male guests usually act as auxiliary cooks and waiters. Extra help may not be necessary, but at large cookouts a professional organizer in the kitchen, arranging platters and putting leftovers away, is worth the price.

The Cook Is Not in the Kitchen

For those who have neither the time nor inclination to handle the cooking and serving themselves, and who have no in-home help, there are amateurs and experts available for hire, and they range all the way from high-school students to highly experienced chefs. Besides, it is no longer necessary to cook, unless you enjoy it. Food in finished form can be purchased today from supermarkets as well as from the growing number of takeout establishments. And if time or inclination prevents you from even the effort of finding help, or shopping for prepared food, a caterer can relieve you of almost all responsibility.

More often than not I do abdicate my role of chef and waitress. I am convinced that when I take to the kitchen I am capable of arousing jealousy in the bosoms of chefs at any three-star restaurant; the problem is that I so rarely have the time or the materials to produce convincing evidence. Company coming, particularly of the last-minute variety, always seems to coincide with an office emergency, or a Mother Hubbard crisis; that is, the cupboard is bare of the ingredients necessary for the special dish I have in mind.

My family remains skeptical of my culinary prowess, but they have had a good many convincing examples of my ability to cope with crises. For instance, on a recent Sunday afternoon we received a call from some Swedish friends who had just arrived in New York and were leaving the next day. They wanted to see us and our home and they also wanted to see three other couples who had visited them in Sweden. There was only one possible answer: takeout food.

Randy and I raced to a nearby establishment known by the happy name of The Chirping Chicken. With four grilled birds, neatly cut into sixteen portions and nestling in a sack next to pita bread, salsa, and a large container of coleslaw, we stopped briefly to pick up strawberry ice cream, frozen berries, and fancy packaged cookies.

I had some oranges and two cans of cranberry sauce in the house. The chickens were distributed on platters and surrounded by orange and cranberry slices, with sprigs of parsley tucked between. The coleslaw went into a large bowl and I added a sliced tomato as decoration. The by-now softened ice cream was spooned into a melon mold and placed in the freezer. When we were ready for dessert it looked quite handsome, unmolded on our best Limoges platter and glazed with a sauce of melted strawberries.

When there is no cook in the kitchen, and when you have been working overtime in the office or have failed to find a satisfactory substitute, there are always takeout stores and even supermarket shelves full of items that require few additional touches to make them appear home-concocted. Several years ago we entertained some guests from Chicago and I remembered at the last minute that they once told us they "simply adored" East Coast seafood. It was too late to change the entire menu, which included no seafood, but I did substitute Campbell's New England Clam Chowder for the melon I had planned as the first course, adding a dollop of whipped cream and minced chives. My friend took one taste of the soup and said, "This is absolutely wonderful. You can certainly tell the real thing! This is the kind of chowder that we can't get in Chicago." I refrained from telling her that she could, indeed, get exactly the same soup in Chicago, and I have felt both triumphant and guilty ever since.

The Restaurant Comes Home

When even picking up food at a takeout store or shopping at the last minute for clam chowder is too much trouble, we order food to be delivered from a nearby restaurant. Many restaurants offer takeout menus and have messengers eager to deliver any order on short notice. As a result of a recent experience, however, I have learned to limit the number of different items I order, no matter how large a group we are feeding.

Last April I was celebrating my birthday by giving myself a party; we had invited the whole family, and I was looking forward to catching up on the details of their busy lives. Unfortunately, I made the serious mistake of asking in advance what particular dish each of them preferred from the neighborhood Chinese restaurant. Dinner arrived in twenty-seven different cartons, and I spent the evening in the kitchen, unpacking, dishing out, carrying in, carrying back to the kitchen, and repacking for storing in the refrigerator. Randy says it was a lovely party.

There are some restaurants whose owners may be willing to act as caterers and to handle everything from preparing the food to serving it. Particularly, ethnic restaurants such as Thai, Japanese, Chinese, and Indian can often provide everything you need to give a party with a special foreign theme, but the selection of a restaurant requires caution. For my oldest son's birthday, recently, we made the mistake of ordering dinner from a restaurant manager for whom this was a first. For us, it became a last.

Because of my son's passion for hot food (hot not in temperature but in pepper), we decided to have an Indian party, completed with costumed waiters and blistering curries. We arranged with the manager of a neighborhood Indian restaurant to cater the dinner at a reasonable price, perhaps too reasonable in retrospect. The evening arrived and so did the guests. By eight o'clock they had been drinking for half an hour, with no food in sight. A call to the restaurant elicited a response in calm, unhurried tones, that "is coming now." By nine o'clock, "now" had come and gone. Randy and I were stationed at the back door waiting for the elevator to disgorge our Indians. At nine-thirty, with a houseful of overmellowed guests, five waiters in costume, carrying trays and boxes of food emptied out of the elevator. One of them informed us pleasantly, "No more customer in restaurant, so we come."

The food was plentiful, and the sharpened appetites made it doubly delicious. We learned, however, to make more than doubly sure that a restaurant is experienced at catering parties and that the owner understands quite clearly what is expected.

Extra Hired Hands

When the number of guests exceeds six, we hire outside help. If we are giving a large reception or cocktail party, the help includes a professional bartender and, depending on the size of the event, professional waiters or waitresses. I have learned the importance of this kind of assistance from observing parties where people were lined up six deep at a barely functioning bar, and where almost all the canapés were still in the kitchen after the guests had gone.

If you are not one of the fortunate few who have regular help available, there are many sources of good party help. There are catering establishments that do not require you to buy a whole catering package, if all you need is a bartender. And many local colleges have employment bureaus that refer students who are trained to handle parties. If you employ a student you will not only get an eager helper, but you will be providing a young person with an opportunity to earn badly needed funds. They may not be as professional as the caterer-supplied help, but they make up for this by being grateful for the work and therefore more obliging.

In some cities where there is an active theater community, young actors and actresses waiting for casting opportunities are often glad to accept "parts" as helpers. In New York a number of the better-known caterers depend entirely on thespian help. But perhaps the best source of information about party help is a friend whom you trust, although even good friends have been known to conceal this type of precious information. Still, if you observe the performance of an effective caterer or waitress at someone else's home, you might ask the hosts whether they are willing to give you the name of, or permit you to speak to, their employee. Obviously it is rude to do this without permission.

Many of my friends prefer the ease that results from hiring a caterer who will provide everything, including the food, the equipment, and the help. Assuming that the party has been planned in advance, and that you do not have the time or the inclination to bother with shopping or last-minute platter arranging, or that the party will be too large to be managed by amateurs, and also assuming that cost is not a major object, caterers are a marvelous resource. I have used a caterer from time to time, with happy results and in only one instance a less-than-felicitous outcome. I had failed to discuss details in advance and the caterer, having misunderstood the plans, provided one bartender for a cocktail party of more than a hundred thirsty guests, most of whom went home still thirsty. I learned from that experience to make every expectation specific.

Caterers vary in ability, menus, and prices. When they are good, the food they offer is almost invariably more remarkable, more glamorous, and more exotic than anything that most home cooks can manage. If you have dealt with one person or company over a period of time, you may feel safe merely saying, "There will be twelve for dinner at eight, and I leave the arrangements to you." I have never felt quite that safe, and it is always better to discuss the arrangements in detail.

Most guests today can tell that a meal has been catered, and sometimes even who the caterer is. However, caterers do enable working families to entertain attractively, with little effort or stress. Platters are apt to look beautiful but a little contrived, unless you make it very plain that you prefer home style. Also, you may wish to request that the caterer or the assistant not insist on selecting the type or amount of food for those guests who wish to serve themselves.

In hiring a catering service, a friend's recommendation is invaluable. Selecting someone on the basis of an ad is risky. A friend of ours hired a Japanese caterer from a magazine ad, knowing no more than the ad stated. On the night of the dinner a sumo-wrestler character arrived, who announced that he was in charge of the food. He appeared to take an immediate dislike to the hostess and extended his negative feelings to her guests. The drinks before dinner were glacially slow in arriving, and tropically warm. The hors d'oeuvres, balls of sticky rice, were passed once, which was satisfactory, since no one was tempted to finish the first. Finally, when dinner was announced, guests found at each place a small plate with pieces of chicken threaded on two toothpicks; these were disposed of in a very few minutes. The plates were replaced by small cups of very sour grapefruit sorbet. "Ah," said one of the guests, "a palate cleanser—but a little early, isn't it, for cleansing the palate?" "I hope it's not dessert," said the hostess, not too hopefully.

In due course, demitasse cups of coffee were delivered to each of us, and there was no longer any doubt that dinner was over. My friend was a perfect hostess. She laughed—the laughter was a little strained—went to her refrigerator, and returned with some cheese and a box of strawberries, which all the guests shared. In between bites of cheese, the hostess confessed that she had not checked the caterer's credentials, nor obtained the menu in writing.

My friend's sad experience fortunately is not a common one and, in any case, it is easy to avoid. All that is required is a little research; and if you are using the the services of a particular caterer for the first time, ask for a written contract, with a warning that payment of the bill will depend on fulfilling the contract. In fact, it is a good idea to get everything in writing, even if the caterer is your son-in-law. Perhaps a written contract is even more important in that circumstance.

The Well-Staffed Affair

Competent live-in help makes entertaining easy, although even they may fail at times. One friend of ours, whose household usually runs elaborately and well, faced an interesting dilemma at a dinner she gave in honor of an ambassador. There was a crash in the kitchen followed by a lengthy pause, before her very loyal live-in butler entered with the first course, a platter surmounted by a somewhat haphazard mound of salmon mousse. Instead of serving the hostess first, which was his wont, the butler passed the platter to each of the guests. Finally reaching his employer, he whispered, "Madam, the cook dropped the salmon and there may be some glass in it, so we wouldn't want *you* to eat it."

There are moments when even the best-trained crew in the kitchen may leave the host no recourse except to discourage guests from partaking of a particular dish, with the hope that they are either not very hungry or that they have senses of humor. The only inviolable rule is never to instruct or criticize help during the course of a meal. We have always dreaded going to a certain home where the hostess corrects those who are serving her in an unending sotto-voce monologue. The problem is that the monologue is not as sotto as she intends, and it effectively stultifies conversation. One must endure mistakes, and correct them later, but never in front of guests.

Of course, if you have your own live-in help, or if you have someone who comes to your home on a fairly regular basis whenever you have company, or who works for you and some of your friends even occasionally, entertaining becomes relatively simple.

A little while ago we received a call from a good friend. "I'm having the Buhlers on the eighteenth of March," she said. "Can you and Randy come for dinner?" Her tone made me feel that it would be gauche to inquire who the Buhlers were. I knew they must be very important, that I should have recognized their names, and that they probably came from England where my friend knew a positive gaggle of dukes and duchesses. Of course we accepted, and we looked forward to meeting the Buhlers.

On the night of the party no unknown guests appeared, but we felt that it might be tactless to inquire as to the whereabouts of the Buhlers. It was a lovely evening with beautiful food beautifully presented. It was not until I actually met the Buhlers—a remarkable couple, very much in demand—at someone else's home a few months later that I realized they had been responsible for the meal and service at my friend's home. Smart lady! Her party had been planned to coincide with the availability of the fabulous Buhlers.

Before the first invitation goes out, the ducks, even if they are not on the dinner menu, should be all in a row. Unless you are planning to do all the work, the most important ducks are the counterparts of the Buhlers, the efficient, quiet, and pleasant experts who will enable you to enjoy your own party. If you know and can afford the Buhlers, I suggest that you clear a date with them before you even think of a guest list.

6

Stage Settings

Decorations and Equipment

We scoured the market for dishes and glasses
And silver and linen. Now bring on the masses.

I believe that the ambience of a party is as important to its success as the food and service. This does not have to mean elegant appointments, or a house that is a mansion rather than a home, but it does imply that everything from the table setting to the soap in the guest bathroom should show thought and care for the guests' comfort. The atmosphere, from the mood set by the table decorations to the general appearance of the rooms, informs a guest either that he is important—or that his hosts consider him comparable to an old shoe. Guests' attitudes can be irrevocably influenced by the perceived attitudes of their hosts.

On the other hand, a home should not look as though an interior designer had just closed the front door on the way out, and as though moving a single ashtray would violate some great scheme. I have a friend who so loves the arrangement of her living room that she actually once reprimanded a guest for moving a chair in order to join a group. She thus violated the most basic rule of hospitality: Never scold a guest in your home unless his actions threaten arson. And never value a piecrust table on which a guest has placed a wet-bottomed glass more than you value his or her friendship. It is always possible to move a glass quietly or place it on a coaster without comment.

Making the House Guest-Inspectable

Any room that will be exposed to public scrutiny requires your private scrutiny before the party. Each time I give my room a pre-party once-over I am haunted by the disapproving spectre of my mother and a sense that the apartment must somehow be shaped up to meet her demanding standards. Randy and I use a corner of our bedroom as an at-home office, and it is generally swamped by clippings, periodicals, unanswered invitations, requests for funds, and bills, all waiting obtrusively for attention. Before each party the debris on the desk is stashed underneath, or disposed of in a closet, always in careful order so that it can be retrieved logically the next day. There is a risk of a guest blundering into the closet on the way to the bathroom, but it's a risk one has to take if a room has been cleared by the stash-away method.

The bathroom requires extra attention. There should be a cake of unused hand soap, a bottle of lotion, perfume, or toilet water available, as well as sufficient guest towels, including some for show and paper ones that will actually be used. I find that guests either emerge with wet hands or use a bath mat when the only choice is our best lace-and-linen finger towels.

The rest of the house should be given equal attention, and that includes the kitchen. We seem to keep piles of old newspapers in a corner of the kitchen, neatly stacked but not particularly eye-appealing. Occasionally guests may have to enter through the kitchen, and so we arrange for a face-lift, which means moving the papers to the recycling bin the day before the party.

With the background in shining condition, we can turn our attention to the equipment that is needed for the care and feeding of guests.

Collecting the Props

Of all living creatures, from protozoa to primates, *Homo sapiens* is the only species that takes the presentation of food as seriously as its consumption. Whether it is sushi in a lacquer box, caviar in a silver bowl, or chopped chicken liver in the shape of a bride and groom, a pleasingly arranged spread sharpens appetites and adds to the pleasure of a meal. For very large parties it may be necessary to rely on rented plates, glassware, and cutlery, but for smaller groups it is possible, economically sound, and fun, to acquire your own supplies and decorations. It makes entertaining both easier and less expensive, and your table will look more interesting and original.

In order to accumulate attractive linens, glassware, and china, I recommend keeping an eye open for antiques shops and flea markets when traveling, reading ads for secondhand merchandise, and staying alert for unconventional opportunities. Before purchasing anything, however, consider such matters as storage space and comfort. Tables with jutting legs and chairs that threaten to collapse can ruin a party and should be avoided even at bargain rates.

Caterers are an efficient source of equipment and tableware, but for anyone who entertains frequently, or even occasionally, the cost of renting chairs, china, and silverware can be prohibitive. We solved the problem over a period of years through a system of bargain hunting and accruals. Tag sales, secondhand stores, flea markets, and small auction establishments (even at times the great establishments like Christie's and Sotheby's) all offer excellent possibilities. Hunting for bargains is just as much fun if the quarry is one or two wine glasses similar to those you already have as it is if you are looking for an unrecognized Rembrandt. And you are actually liable to find the glasses!

Don't be afraid of auction sales. If you are a neophyte you can check the estimates that reliable auction houses provide in their catalogues, and if you can control your competitive impulses or the feeling that "winning" an article represents a victory at any price, you may emerge with some lovely bargains.

We started accruing or collecting in 1952, because of a special sale at Woolworth's Five and Ten Cent Store in White Plains, New York. (In 1952 merchandise still sold for nickels and dimes.) At that time my sons were away at college, but not infrequently they came home for weekends, bringing a large percentage of their friends and acquaintances with them. Our house, which had originally been a barn, and was christened by humorist-publisher Bennett Cerf with the congruous name of "Barn Yesterday," had a separate wing that had once been a chicken house, and could accommodate up to twenty sleeping bags on the floor. On one particular morning I counted that number, all in addition to my sons, who were, as usual, comfortably curled up in their respective beds. With such unanticipated hordes likely to appear at meals during weekends, I kept large quantities of orange juice, eggs, and milk in the refrigerator, and a freezerful of chickens and vegetables ready for quick conversion to casseroles. Dishes and glassware, however, were a constant problem. By 1952, thanks to pretty constant use, most of them were chipped, cracked, and far more limited in quantity than were the guests.

When Woolworth's announced a clearance of pressed-glass plates, cups, and saucers at five cents per item, I rounded up some unwilling assistants and cleaned out the glass-tableware section of the store, thus acquiring the wherewithal to serve the preprandial and prandial appetites of a substantial section of the Yale community. It was a brilliant investment! I have used the glassware at buffet suppers, and each time I think with pleasure of the total cost—under fifteen dollars for eight dozen of each. Packed tightly in cartons and stored out of sight, they have been available when needed ever since. To add to my sense of triumph I have recently seen similar pieces at antiques shows, described as art-nouveau antiques, and priced at seventy-five dollars for one cup and saucer.

After this first successful venture into the home-catering field, I began collecting in earnest. We added flatware next; not fine stainless and certainly not sterling, although the latter can be picked up a few pieces at a time. Instead we started buying plated-silver sets that resemble the real thing. Unless we have guests who make a fetish of examining silver marks (and I have only one friend who falls into that category), people do not seem to notice the difference between the antique sterling we inherited from Randy's uncle and the Macy's, "$50 complete table setting for eight including hostess set." The silver plate will wear off eventually, but that will be a problem for my children. Meanwhile, I can serve sixty or more guests at a tea, a cocktail party, or a buffet supper without incurring the cost of rentals. And I should mention that our sporadic and random purchasing has not been so haphazard as to result in odd or clashing patterns, but what we believe to be a pleasant harmony of designs.

Perhaps my best purchase was three sturdy restaurant-type tables, each large enough for ten people. They are indispensable to us as well as to a number of families who live in our apartment building, and who borrow one or more of the tables whenever their guests exceed the capacity of their permanent seating arrangements. If you know the owners of any restaurants, and they are inclined to be friendly, they may help you locate a supply house or even be willing to place an order for you. We found our way to the source through the good offices of Mr. Jerry Berns, an erstwhile owner of The '21' Club in New York.

At the same time that the tables moved in with us, we found a dozen stacking chairs on a sidewalk outside a wholesale-retail house in lower Manhattan. These are finished in a sort of antique gold, with padded seats and backs in a color that blends in with that of our regular dining-room chair seats. Not collector's items in the usual sense, but certainly an improvement over folding chairs. They have joined the tables in our basement storage area.

Storing the Props

It seems superfluous to mention that in order to keep a reserve of equipment and furniture it is necessary to find sufficient storage space. Still, many potential hoarders of extra supplies fail to recognize that they have "superfluous" or unused corners, shelves, and invisible areas capable of providing a home for infrequently used items. A careful search can turn up some interesting and unusual storage possibilities.

For residents of studio and efficiency apartments, locating areas to store extra plates and glassware, let alone tables and chairs, is virtually impossible. Fortunately, the number of guests who can be accommodated in one-room apartments makes hoarding of more than a few items unnecessary. Those who live in larger quarters may find it easier to be inventive in finding storage. Since extra supplies are used only occasionally, they can be stashed in inconvenient and hard-to-reach places: in flat cartons under beds, behind the sofa, under a table, or on an extra shelf built at the very top of a closet. We keep flower containers under a sink, and a friend of ours has found a small hiding place behind drapes in the living room. It should be noted that a random scattering of little objects in various storage spaces may result in forgetting what has been stored, and where. If possible, there should be a system, or at least a list, so that extra glasses, trays, and holiday decorations are readily retrievable.

Of course, if you have storage space in a basement, or obliging relatives with attics, the problem is solved. But no matter how little space you need, or how much you are able to locate, there is one process vital to storing equipment and supplies, and that is, quite simply, the ongoing activity of discarding excess and obsolete possessions periodically.

Setting the Table

Assuming that all the correct utensils are available, the table for a formal dinner should be set at least half a day in advance, and preferably the night before. That way, if it is discovered that there is one less fork than person, there is still time for remedy.

My mother-in-law owned a silver chest that stood on the floor and contained two dozen each of some fourteen different types of forks, knives, and spoons. There were oyster forks, fish forks, dessert forks, teaspoons, coffee spoons, dessert spoons, salad forks, consommé spoons, soup spoons, tablespoons, and knives for every type of course, including some I could not identify. Fortunately we no longer endure ten-course meals and, except in rare circumstances like a dinner for the Chevaliers de Tastevins or some other wine society, elaborate table settings have become obsolete. It is fun to contemplate my mother-in-law's world, to remember the different glasses needed for various wines, the heavy silver centerpieces requiring endless polishing, the silver platters and salvers and trays on which the food was served. Setting the table was laborious. Today it is creative and fun.

At formal parties I use my mother's candelabras, and a Chinese-export tureen as a centerpiece, with several small flower arrangements in bowls spaced down the center of the table. For an indoor clambake with lobster and corn, however, we use red checked tablecloths and mugs for beer, or newspapers covered with fishnets.

Rich and expensive tablecloths are charming, and require care to maintain. With a little ingenuity and very little talent, a lovely tablecloth or one that is interesting and suited to a particular occasion can be created inexpensively, or found at sales.

One solution is a paper tablecloth, which is ideal for children's parties when the spills are liable to be excessive, and for outdoor picnics where informality is appropriate. On most other occasions I prefer something a little more substantial.

At brunches and luncheons, place mats are my choice. Several sets of lace and embroidered-linen table mats were included in my long-ago trousseau, and some of them survive today. When friends of my own generation come for lunch the good lace mats are brought out.

The rest of the time I use cork, wood, and colorful plastic mats that can be wiped off rather than having to be laundered. In other words, the time of day and the formality of the occasion determine the table setting. Still, anything that adds to the work of entertaining detracts from the joy, and contemplating extensive laundering is joyless.

For dinner parties I take the best tablecloths out of the linen closet, and I accept the fact that there will be a price to pay for their use. The extra laundering is worthwhile, compensated for by our guests' appreciation. For very formal dinners I use damask, lace, or embroidered organdy; the old-fashioned kind of which my mother would have approved. Two that I treasure were made by my grandmother of lace pieced together in intricate designs, with the tiniest of stitches, and steeped in light tea to simulate the antique tint that by now they would have acquired naturally. Cloths like these appear at auction sales from time to time, so anyone who has not inherited an heirloom tablecloth can still own one. We keep ours in black tissue paper in a long box so that the creases will not become sharp. It may be more practical to buy lace curtain material, hem the edges, and dip the finished cloth in weak tea or coffee. The result is an instant heirloom, and one is spared the agony (always endured in silence!) when a guest spills half a glass of wine on a genuine antique.

And for those special birthdays and holidays I have created tablecloths, using unbleached muslin, and writing with indelible marking pens of different colors the names of family and friends who are apt to attend. I have recently added the names of my new granddaughters-in-law, and eventually I hope to add the names of great-grandchildren. Everyone seems to enjoy seeing their names, and I have even had distressed tycoons circling the table, unwilling to find their seats until they have located their names somewhere on the tablecloth.

For those with artistic talent, a tablecloth is a wonderful canvas, if you can overcome the lessons of childhood regarding graffiti on walls and linens.

Lighting

Candlelight is romantic, but most of us are accustomed to electric lights, and we may have trouble seeing what we are eating if lights are too low. On the other hand, very bright light can seem garish, and most of us do look better in soft light. While I don't recommend rewiring, I do recommend investing in dimmers.

Lighting is very much part of a decorating scheme, and candles and candelabra make a table look attractive, even if the flowers are sparse. Of course, candles are not appropriate at luncheons, but for evening parties they are essential. One important consideration is to avoid having the candlelight at eye level. It is distracting for guests to talk across a table through a flickering flame that obscures the other people, just as flowers at the wrong level can be more irritating than lovely.

Small containers such as those used in restaurants can look enchanting placed at intervals down the length of a table, and very tall candles give a table an air of dignity. There are so many different sizes and types of candles that a hostess has a wide choice. At Christmas we may use conventional red candles, or the very thick kind that my Swedish friends send us, or even a jolly red Santa Claus with a wick coming out of his cap.

There are times when only candlelight with no additional electric lighting is appropriate. Romantic dinners for two should not stop once two people have each said "I do." They are lovely for anniversaries and just for the no-occasion moments when you feel romantic. Send the children to Grandma's for the night, turn out the lights, light the candles, and put a disc with your favorite song on whatever machine you use.

I suggest that you check your plans with Grandma first. She may be planning a candlelight supper for two on the same night.

And Finally

Is it possible to give a successful party with no decorations, with plastic tableware and plates, and in a home that has not been redecorated in twenty years? Of course! An informal group of drop-ins with a feast of deli sandwiches can make a great party. Besides, worrying visibly about the way a table or a room looks is apt to ruin a party faster than appearances ever could. Just as a dinner for two will depend for success less on the color of the candles than on the mood of the participants and the after-dinner activities, so it is for a gathering of twenty or more. (Although the after-dinner activities are undoubtedly different in the two cases.)

I try to have the right accoutrements in the right quantities, and I try to limit our guest list to fit the glassware, but if I have to wash some of the glasses between courses, or if I am a little short of any item, I have learned not to look concerned. No matter what else is forgotten, a smile and the rules of hospitality make a setting complete.

7

The Last Roundup

Preparty Planning

I test the equipment, leave nothing to fate
I count every fork, every glass, every plate
I look at the seating and change every card
I study the linen by inch and by yard
An item neglected I failed to inspect?
Make a note, recollect it, and next time correct.
A flaw undetected? Too much of a hurry?
No problem. No matter. Big deal. Not to worry!

Recently I arranged for the delivery of a ten-pound, cooked and decorated salmon as the main course for dinner. At six-thirty when I realized it hadn't arrived, I called our fish store. Too late! The store was obviously closed, the salmon was obviously not swimming in our direction, it was now almost seven o'clock, and in a few minutes guests would be arriving for a virtually nonexistent dinner. Randy, always calm in such situations, pointed out that my threatened suicide would provide guests with a topic of conversation but would not improve the party as a whole. Three packages of hot dogs and a similar number of rolls that had been purchased for a family gathering on the next Sunday became our dinner, and no one starved. In fact, one of the guests subsequently sent me a charming thank-you card with a picture of two fish hugging each other, under the heading, "Salmon chanted evening."

On the morning after the hot-dog fiasco I received an aggrieved and apologetic message from the fish-store owner, with the somewhat mysterious explanation that my order had become "attached to Mrs. Pincus." At the same time I learned, or relearned, an important lesson: Any last-minute deliveries should be reconfirmed a few hours before a party, and all other details should be checked in advance.

Parties that are put together at the last moment, and with the simplest kind of food, can be delightful. Still, planning ahead has advantages, even if the food and service are both quite simple, the guests understanding, and the hosts secure enough to be untroubled by the possibility of running out of liquor or forgetting to pick up dessert.

From time to time we have had a hundred or more guests at parties or fund-raising events for causes. Organizing the menu and the equipment is boiler-plate simple, if and when I follow a kind of previewing plan: At the conclusion of a previous party I have made a mental note of problems, and an actual note of any equipment that may need attention or replacement; I keep a manila folder with menus I have used at past parties, with shopping lists for each, ready to be exhumed and revitalized at future parties. In accordance with my previous recommendations I try to hire help who have worked for me before and who are therefore familiar with the where and what of our home. On the day before the party I open one of the bottles of wine I plan to serve, to avoid having a poorly aged vintage compete with the salad dressing. And of course I now know that I must call during the afternoon to ensure that Mrs. Pincus will not receive the fish I expect to serve for dinner that night.

It is true that even my best-laid plans "gang aft agley"—well, maybe not so "aft," but certainly once in a while. Without any preplanning, however, the small catastrophes are liable to occur more than once in a while. For instance, even though the wine may be at its peak, a shortage of wine glasses, requiring the use of tumblers, will have an adverse effect on the bouquet; the curried lamb, untested in advance, may be helplessly bland because the amount of curry powder was seriously underestimated; and the guests at a formal dinner may mill around aimlessly when dinner is announced looking for places to sit because the place cards are still in the stationery store.

To avoid postparty regrets it is useful to keep notes on the items to be checked, based on unfortunate previous experiences. There may be an excuse for having one party with no vodka in the house, but as I gently reminded Randy, who is responsible for all purchases of alcoholic supplies, there is no excuse for a repetition of the same situation the following week. New equipment should never be used for the first time when you have guests, and unless your name is Julia Child, you should avoid serving a dish that has never been tried before.

The Plan of Attack

An authentic, old-fashioned formal dinner, or a semiformal buffet supper, requires a tactical approach similar to the planning of army maneuvers. When we moved into our first apartment I asked our new general housekeeper-cook-and-waitress to prepare a meal that included a last-minute fish course, a roast beef, potatoes au gratin in a casserole, and a chocolate soufflé, all in one small oven. She spent the afternoon packing. Since then I have been conscious of the fact that if dinner is to be served without endless pauses between courses, I must consider counter space, oven capacity, and the ability of my armed forces. Organizing a dinner does not call for the skill and acumen of a brigadier general, but it does require a knowledge of kitchen logistics.

Preplanning need not be a cumbersome project, but if you are using a caterer for the first time, you may want not only to review the menu but actually to sample the food that is to be served. If the microwave oven is new, you will want to try it at least once before D day. And if the help you will depend on is inexperienced, you may wish to spend some time in advance showing and telling them what you expect.

On one New Year's Eve that none of my eight guests will ever allow me to forget I cooked a chicken on a brand-new electric rotisserie (an untried-until-then Christmas present). When I brought the finished (and very finished it was) bird to the table there was a pregnant pause, broken finally by one lady who said, in awestruck tones, "Good Heavens! A giant toasted marshmallow!" Subsequently, my rotisserie and I became friends, and I learned about timing. On that evening of its debut, however, we started the New Year with unsatisfied appetites.

Similarly, a friend of ours last Thanksgiving Day, having invited twenty-two for dinner, helplessly watched her well-burnished turkeys resting inside a convection oven whose door no one was able to open. The serviceman, who knew the secret, arrived the next day, opened the oven, and recommended that the turkeys be buried with honors.

Inventory

Preplanning includes checking table linens to be sure they haven't collected mold or become dirty around the edges; polishing silverware; counting glasses; rinsing demitasse cups that have become dusty; organizing a seating plan; and, in fact, reviewing every aspect of the forthcoming party. Some of this can be cursory and even omitted by hosts who give parties regularly. Still, a certain amount of prechecking is wise. The disposal may have devoured some of the silverware since the last party, and other items may have become undependable. You can positively count on the gradual disappearance of cocktail napkins that resemble handkerchiefs. (Paper napkins may not be as impressive, but they are practical.)

Checking should include a mental preview of the evening's activities. For instance, when guests arrive on a cold wintry night they will need a place to deposit their coats. Depending on the size of the party I make sure that a rack or sufficient hangers in a closet are available to accommodate all the expected coats. The mishandling of outerwear can be a source of irritation to guests. I believe that some of the pleasure of an evening can be dissipated by a treasure hunt at the end, if one is forced to claw desperately through mountains of clothing. Helping to shed and eventually to retrieve coats is part of the service good hosts owe their guests.

Some preplanning can be eliminated if you have been observant at a previous party and so have identified deficiencies that may need to be remedied before the next event. And if you are an experienced host or hostess, you have probably produced a number of similar events in the past and you have undoubtedly established a satisfactory system, so that rehearsals for subsequent performances can be perfunctory.

Of course, previewing is not always a guarantee of a successful final result. Checking physical conditions, equipment, menus, and other items can only lead to a happy outcome if the original plan is well-conceived. One of my more thoroughly planned parties was a bridge event with several tables of players. They were to change partners after each round. The result was that, during the entire party, everyone seemed to be rushing wildly from table to table. Worst of all, by the end of the evening the master score, for which I assumed responsibility, was as confused and confusing as the current trade deficit. It was impossible to award prizes, and it was even more impossible to appease the couple who assumed they had won. My plans were too complicated and obviously beyond my capacity to implement.

The processes of planning may seem tedious, but traversing the swamp of a totally unplanned event makes preparty tedium more than worthwhile. I have one friend of whom I remain fond, merely because our relationship dates back to kindergarten. She specializes in nonplanning, and as a result the receipt of her invitations evokes more dread than pleasurable anticipation. For instance, seating is never arranged, and as a result at a recent party one man wandered around the table, looking unhappily for a place to sit, and found the only remaining spot between two other men; at which point the agitated hostess moved everybody out of their seats in an effort to remedy the situation, thereby creating at least five minutes of chaos. On another occasion she served cornish hens, rather tastelessly prepared, and one fewer than the total number of guests. To compound the lack of planning, she recognizes and is made unhappy by flaws and mishaps, and as a result her guests are equally unhappy. It is sad to spend the evening worrying, when a small amount of before-the-fact attention could result in both the hostess and her guests having fun. And yet the fact that she makes the effort to entertain at all means that her friends do overlook the flaws, return, albeit reluctantly, and invite her to all their parties, thus proving, one more time, that giving even an unplanned party makes better sense than sitting home alone.

8

The Main Event

Orchestrating a Dinner

With our guests still standing upright
Long before they get unsteady
While they still can hold a cup right
We announce that dinner's ready
Maybe formal or self-service!
And no matter what occurs
We are never ever nervous.
I just smile and Randy purrs.

Randy and I discarded the commitment to perfection in entertaining rather early in our married life, but we still enjoy some of the traditional formality that we learned long ago, especially at dinner parties. Today we give buffet suppers more frequently than formal dinners, and we are aware that most of our younger friends associate seated and served affairs with weddings, parties for visiting royalty, and benefits at large hotels.

My mother would have considered the current hotel banquets nothing less than appalling, particularly those at which the waiters distribute piled-up plates as though they were dealing cards in Las Vegas. My mother-in-law, on the other hand, who was famous for her work in the musical world but disdained conventionalism, taught me that deviations from Emily Post's bible might actually add to the pleasure of the guests. There is a lot to be said in favor of simplicity, augmented by a few special touches, such as attractively arranged platters, carefully planned seating, and a good, not great, California wine. And if work can be lessened by home-style service, or by passing plates down to the hostess for removal at the end of a course, then by all means let the hosts dish up the food and collect the empties at the end of the meal. Just don't invite Emily Post!

There are, however, times when formality is not only appropriate but a pleasant departure from today's blue-jean world. Formal dinners demand a special effort to look one's best, and that applies to hosts as well as guests. A roomful of people, all of whom are feeling pleased with their appearance, and most of whom, in fact, look better than usual, is guaranteed to create a party mood. On the other hand, there is no reason why festive or even formal attire is not appropriate for buffets, particularly if guests are seated at tables.

Seating Plans

Preparing place cards, or determining who and how you will want to bring guests together in a group during and after dinner if there is no formal seating arrangement, is one of the final party activities before the guests arrive. It plays a large role in the ultimate success of an event and should be given thought and time.

Randy is helpful in this area of planning. He is always ready to offer advice on the aspects of seating arrangements that deal with comfort, although he never shares my interest in the potential for matchmaking. He will point out the danger of seating our son's college basketball team on small folding chairs. I, on the other hand, always imagine the various subjects guests might find in common to discuss and their political compatibility as well as other potential forms of compatibility. My assessments have not been inevitably successful, and at times when I have forced Randy to focus on my concerns the results have been quite salutory, proving again that two minds are better then one.

Seating logistics may require mathematical calculations. If there is an even number of males and females, and if the table is oblong, the numbers eight, twelve, and sixteen make it impossible for the host and hostess to occupy the seats at the two ends of the table unless two men and two women are placed next to each other. Try it! You will find that it is simpler to invite ten or fourteen, unless of course your dining-room table is round. When we have eight or twelve guests, Randy sits at the head of the table and I sit on the side next to a gentleman who occupies the end seat. There are other solutions that we have tried, including sitting opposite each other in the center of the table or avoiding a precise male-female match. To keep things simple I prefer inviting the right number of guests.

Among our friends, women outnumber men. We invite our single female friends even if two women will have to sit next to each other. It seems ridiculous to worry about achieving symmetry when too often we are omitting someone whose company we truly enjoy in favor of a gentleman who does not talk, let alone sing, for his supper. Even at the most formal dinners it is acceptable to place two ladies next to each other. I do try to ensure that each guest has at least one partner who is amusing, and I assign major clunkers to Randy and myself.

If the party consists of two couples in addition to Randy and me, the seating plan is obvious. When the number exceeds six, I prepare a seating list in advance, which I then conceal in the front of my dress and which often slips out of reach. For larger parties I use monogrammed place cards, with the names carefully written or printed; except that occasionally I liven up the search for seats by having pen-and-ink cartoons, quotations from Bartlett's, or limericks, instead of, or in addition to, the names.

Saving and reusing cards is one of my economies, but I am careful to write on only one side. At an ex-friend's home some time ago, when conversation had ground to a halt, I turned my card over and discovered another name on the back. There proved to be names on the back of all the cards, and the guests had a lovely time reconstructing the earlier party, which we decided had been our hostess's "A" group. She was not amused, and in fact my card was never used again.

The writing on a place card should be legible to the hosts when they stand behind the chairs before the guests arrive. If not, the cards should be rewritten. It is not fair to require myopic guests to grope for glasses or to request assistance in reading. Incidentally, it is permissible to inform guests who seem to be spending the cocktail hour together that they will be next to each other at dinner and that perhaps they may wish to talk to other friends before they are seated. However, the fact that they have been attracted to each other during the predinner period is a compliment to the hosts' seating perspicacity.

Welcoming the Guests

Whether the dinner is to be served formally or buffet-style, Randy and I are in place, fully dressed at seven-thirty, and waiting for the doorbell to ring. Actually we do not expect anyone to appear until quarter to eight, but there is often one exception, and this exception coincides with the times when we have somehow been unduly delayed. At seven-twenty-nine and a half, when Randy is wrestling with a tuxedo tie and I am struggling with a recalcitrant zipper, the doorbell rings. A gentleman who has no wife to instruct him in social intercourse has arrived precisely to the minute. Inevitably he will remark that he is the first, which is evident, and we respond breathlessly that it is delightful to have time for a chat with our dear friend before the others arrive. I conceal the fact that Randy will finish zipping my dress later, when it can be done inconspicuously. In the meantime we play the role of hosts, making him feel welcome, wanted, and comfortable.

Sometimes we are quite ready at seven-fifteen. At such times, for no fathomable reason, everyone arrives late. Watching the clock and waiting is nerve-wracking and apt to result in a kind of Stella Dallas paranoia, or a transitory case of the "Nobody Loves Me" syndrome. "What if no one comes?" I ask Randy. "What will I do with all that food? What can I say to André (our regular hired bartender)?" At such moments Randy is wont to make matters worse by saying, cheerfully, "Wouldn't it be wonderful if no one showed up and we could have the evening alone?"

I should have learned by now that the people who have accepted our invitation will all arrive, and nearly on time, although there are some exceptions. We have friends who are chronically late, and we have learned to accept that they will appear eventually. Less often a guest may be substantially delayed. Before they make their apologetic entrances, I am liable to become a little anxious, which I like to interpret as a symptom of caring, but which is probably the result of having been less organized than I consider advisable. Have they forgotten? Did I forget to invite them in the first place? Should I try to reach them by phone and if they don't answer should I assume they're on their way to our home, or to some other place? If the latter, should I reset the table and try to reconstruct a reasonable seating plan?

On what are, thankfully, very rare occasions, a guest has actually failed to appear by the time word comes from the kitchen that dinner is ready. In that infrequent case, I remove chairs quietly and we start dinner. Guests who are an hour late and have not notified us by phone may have to face the embarrassment of waiting while their places are reset. While they are in our home, however, we try to behave in accordance with Old Testament hospitality. That means greeting them enthusiastically, revealing that although their places were removed it was with the greatest reluctance, since their presence was absolutely essential to their hosts and to the other guests. No reference to their rude tardiness is allowed, unless they wish to entertain the gathering with an intriguing explanation. The rules of hospitality are immutable. A guest in our home is treasured and made much of, which does not prevent us from removing him, her, or them from future lists.

The Cocktail Hour

The period of time during which guests are assembling requires intensive host activity. Orchestrating the processes of mixing and mingling is fundamental to a successful party, and no single guest should be allowed to sit languishing alone over the crudités. In England I remember spending an entire evening without learning the name or occupation of a single person at a fairly large party. Not so in America! Identification is the first order of business. Who they are and what they do should be warmly and charmingly revealed as hosts present each new arrival. "I want you particularly to meet—" or "I don't think you've met—and you two have so much in common" or "I didn't realize you knew each other, and imagine, you're old friends! What a small world!" Even with guests whom you know are acquainted, a complimentary word or two eases the entry into a group. "Have you had a chance to see Gordon's marvelous documentary about a blind child? It will be on PBS this fall" or "did you know that Louise is about to have one-woman show at the Madison gallery?" or "Have you heard that Janet is our new club champion? She broke the course record last weekend." We never leave the first moments of a party to chance.

Introductions are followed by attention to the provision of drinks and canapés. Most important, we watch to see that all the guests are talking happily to each other. Incidentally, the "hour" should not exceed thirty minutes if friends are on the port side of sixty. Standing for longer than that can be hard on our geriatric crowd, whose shoes tend to start pinching rather earlier than those of our younger friends. Our children and their colleagues can endure a full hour, plus, and when we entertain their generation we do extend the potation period. In any and every instance, however, we remain conscious of individual capacities. Guests who expect to drive home are our responsibility, but even those with limousines and chauffeurs (very rare these days) may become unattractive if they are allowed to reach the silly stage. Bartenders, husbands, and amateur helpers should be repeatedly warned against "slugging," and quietly reminded to water the drinks of guests with low tolerance levels.

When everyone is talking animatedly, Randy and I have sometimes wondered whether we would be missed if we disappeared. Actually, when we are being ignored we are comfortably aware that the party is off to a good start. We can relax until we are needed to marshal the group for the march into dinner.

Dinner

The precise time at which dinner should be announced depends on several factors. Has everyone arrived and should the late guests be given five more minutes to finish their drinks? Are there very few canapés or hors d'oeuvres left and have the platters circulated several times with no takers? Has no one wanted a refill from the bar during the last five minutes, except for a guest who shouldn't have one? Is almost everyone's glass now empty? Ultimately the decision will be heavily influenced by the cook, even if it is the hosts who are responsible for the food preparation. Too long a wait after the dinner is ready to be served may ruin not only the food but, more important, the cook's disposition.

During a formal, seated dinner both Randy and I watch to see that no guests are sitting staring into space because the partners on either side are engaged in conversation with others. Ideally, everyone should change direction between courses, or more frequently, if the service is slow. If they become too absorbed to remember their obligations, the watchful host intervenes. In our home we solve the problem by rapping on a glass (gently, if the glasses are the wedding-gift crystal!) and rising to propose a toast. If this doesn't break up the pattern, we sometimes address a remark, or recall an anecdote to one of the two insouciant partners of the stranded guest.

In addition to helping individual guests remain involved in conversation, we listen to the decibel level. A silent dinner may be a tribute to the soufflé, but it is more liable to be a signal that the social soufflé is collapsing. Randy or I have been known to insert a postdinner-type joke, with some shock value, into a too-lengthy conversational pause; or raise a moderately controversial issue to get the ball bouncing again. No matter how fascinating my partner may be (and I do take the most interesting guest at times, even at the expense of giving two clunkers to a close friend), I believe that a host is always on duty, and it is our responsibility to include others in our conversation.

Buffets

There are advantages that buffets have over formal dinners. People who are not happy with their assigned partners, or who are inadequate at small talk, may get up and circulate a bit. Also, an unexpected guest or a last-minute cancellation will cause less of a problem, particularly if seats are not assigned. Besides, a buffet supper saves labor costs since far less service is required. However, the rules of hospitality are the same, and we follow the same procedures that we would for a formal dinner: meeting and greeting guests, and when supper is announced, helping them to find their seats. After guests have found their assigned places, we invite them to serve themselves. Sometimes we arrange to have the first course on the table, and serve the dessert so that guests must get up only once to help themselves to the main course.

In lieu of a formal seating arrangement, it is wise, if at all possible, to provide small tables where guests can rest their plates while eating. People who are juggling plates full of food, glasses of wine, and collections of silverware are a present danger to the rug, to the other guests, and to themselves. We have small folding tables that we put next to chairs, and when the number of guests will exceed the number of tables, either I serve finger food in bite-size morsels or have edibles so tender they can be cut easily with a fork. Dessert is either similarly bite-size or is passed on individual plates.

Even if guests are experts at balancing plates, they can get tired of standing if there are not enough chairs or sofa seats to accommodate everyone. This is not unusual at cocktail party–buffet combinations. I have found that when all else fails, there is always the floor, except when the majority of the guests are septuagenarians who may have trouble negotiating the up and down aspects without help. Still, the floor is preferable to no seat at all.

On the few occasions when we have had to invite guests to settle on the carpet, we are assiduous about constant cleanup. Discarded plates and glasses and half-filled cups are hazards on that level, or at any level, for that matter.

Even when there is no formal seating plan, I am still a firm advocate of guest geography, which means directing guests to the room, or area of a room, where I believe they will find the most congenial companions. The last time I left the seating purely to chance, I found that the eligible gentleman I invited for a recently divorced and eager lady was sitting in the bedroom next to the most flirtatious married lady at the party. My divorced friend was in the living room sitting with five other ladies.

This does not imply exerting a vigorous kind of control: If in spite of my best efforts a husband and wife go off in a corner by themselves, or if a guest decides to sit in what I consider to be the wrong place, I smile sweetly and start eating. At buffets it is possible to try again later in the meal, by which time a guest may welcome the opportunity to join another group.

Table d'hôte

I have staged some aberrational buffets, which I felt at the time were remarkably creative. One year I gave a series of hor d'oeuvre or smorgasbord parties. I arranged rectangular containers on a table with wheels and offered a large variety of hot and cold dishes. Guests were complimentary and I was exhausted. The labor involved in preparing, serving, and eventually disposing of twenty or more different types of food, from herring to celery-root rémoulade, and from eggs à la russe to Swedish meatballs, was finally overwhelming. The demands of hospitality were neglected in favor of the organizational aspects of the dinner.

At another time I went on a make-it-yourself bender. The buffet table had platters of egg and tuna-fish salads, sliced tomatoes, coleslaw, cheese, a variety of cold cuts, bowls of relish, mayonnaise, and Russian dressing, and thin slices of buttered bread. Guests were encouraged to make their own sandwiches or wait for the frankfurters and hamburgers, which I was creating on a small electric grill in the corner of the dining room. In fact the grill, which had been a Christmas gift, was the impetus for my sandwich obsession. Unfortunately I was able to produce only one hamburger or two hot dogs at a time. The demand was brisk, but the grilling pace was not, and dinner took more time than I like to remember. To compound or exaggerate the problem, I had set up a make-it-yourself sundae bar for dessert. Either dessert or the main course would have been unwieldy. The two together were disastrous. I'm ashamed to say that I learned nothing from the first party and I actually tried the same menu three times before Randy rebelled.

Menus at buffet suppers *can* be innovative without being downright eccentric. Usually I offer more than one main-course choice, and sometimes it is fun to have several varieties of dessert. But any party can be as simple as your time and budget make practical, and guests will remember an attractively presented buffet supper of a casserole, salad, and dessert as fondly as, or perhaps with even more pleasure than, a twelve-course dinner, if the factors that spell hospitality are in place.

Whether the party is a formal seated affair or a find-a-place-and-a-partner buffet, the important factor remains the ability of the hosts to relax and enjoy. Even when the hired butler pours the gravy over the guest of honor, it is essential to stay calm and unruffled. In such circumstances the guest of honor may find it difficult to relax, but since most hired butlers are expert at handling gravy boats, we have been faced with a situation of this type only once, and that was a good many years ago.

Postprandial Precepts

Just as there is an appropriate time for starting dinner, guests should be allowed to escape from the table at an appropriate time. Muscles can get stiff after more than an hour of continuous sitting, and conversations can go stale. Guests should not leave a table before the host or hostess signals the conclusion of the meal by rising, and so Randy and I exchange optical messages that provide agreement on the moment of termination. Randy tends to be more impatient than

I am. If I am still absorbed by an interesting partner, and I continue to ignore the signals, he might finally say, exasperatedly, "Let's get the hell out of here!" Admittedly, this is only after a greatly protracted wait.

The ritual of the ladies withdrawing and the men remaining at table, sipping port, smoking cigars, and discussing the world in Anglo-Saxon words is long past. It is legitimate to invite the ladies to use the bathroom (never "the facilities") and to replace worn lipstick if they wish, and even the gentlemen may want a few minutes to freshen up.

If the ladies become too involved in conversation in the bedroom, I inform them that the men are all in the living room, waiting morosely for them to return. No one believes this, but as a hint it works rather well. By the time the two sexes have rejoined each other the men are usually huddled at one end of the living room discussing Wall Street or the Lakers. It is up to the host and hostess to suggest pleasantly that since this is not a Quaker meeting, they might like to move and make room for a member of the opposite sex.

While people are gathering in the living room we start offering demitasses of coffee (unless it was served at table) with liqueurs or tulipes of champagne, and good conversation. If possible, guests should have a choice of regular or decaffeinated coffee, but if providing that choice is too complicated, only decaf should be served. Once upon a time I went out to the kitchen, as the guests were moving into the living room, and found our pro-tem waitress filling demitasse cups on two separate trays from the same coffee pot. She explained that one tray was for decaf and the other for regular coffee, since "no one knows the difference anyway."

With guests settled in groups, we survey the terrain and suggest to anyone who appears to have wandered into the wrong group, and is looking bored, that he or she might like to join "Dr. so-and-so who is seated in the other room and has been looking forward, I know, to talking with you." And Randy and I join any group that seems to need resuscitation. Also, if it is close to World Series' time, we may invite our male guests, and the few women who are fans, to watch the baseball game on television after dinner, which is the only way I can ensure that Randy will be with at least one group after dinner.

When the meal has lasted longer than usual, guests may stand around talking to each other for a few minutes and then begin the process of thank-yous and good-nights. This does not mean the party is not successful, merely that the hour is late. We are content to allow people to leave while they are still feeling happy, and we never urge them to stay.

In a world of environmental hazards, chemical warfare, and substance abuse, a dinner party, whether conforming to the old-fashioned multi-course and multi-wine tradition or to a simpler and more convenient pattern that fits today's mode, should be gala in feeling; and it should make all of us, hosts and guests, forget the problems of the day while we enjoy the pleasures of the evening.

9

Mishap-pearances

Coping with Unexpected Guests

There's nothing more upsetting
Than the process of forgetting
When I can't remember who or when or what
And there's nothing more appalling
Than the fact of not recalling
What I simply don't remember I forgot
I offer my apology
For disarrayed chronology
Which leads me to behavior misbegotten
And though I know we've never met
You're someone I cannot forget
Unless, alas, you're someone I've forgotten.

No matter how carefully a guest list is compiled, or how vigilantly the entries in a date book are kept, there will probably come a time when someone arrives on the wrong night, or when you appear at the wrong house. You may be sitting in the kitchen with your hair in disarray and with the remains of hamburgers still on the kitchen table when the doorbell rings and there in full party regalia stands a couple you expect for dinner on the same night next week. Or, having written incorrect information in your date book, you arrive fully coiffed at a friend's home to be greeted by their child and informed that his parents went out for dinner thirty minutes ago. Worst of all is the dilemma you could face when you open the front door ready to go out and find a friend whom you really had invited for dinner standing there ready to come in.

There are ways of handling almost any situation, but the guests who appear when I have forgotten completely that they had been invited can constitute a situation that is beyond my capacity to handle. I recall with a sense of horror the times when forgotten guests arrived for dinner. Invariably this occurred when the seating plan had been particularly difficult and when I had spent hours over the placement of each guest, attempting to fit them in physically and also ensure an optimum seating arrangement.

If I can squeeze extra chairs at the already crowded dining-room table I try to get everyone involved in lively conversation at a somewhat extended cocktail hour while we reset the table, but attempting to fit extra guests in physically in two minutes flat is apt to result in the guest of honor sitting somewhere below the salt. Even that is not always possible. In one incredible instance there was simply no more space left for an extra unexpected couple, in either of the two rooms where we had set up tables. Instead, Randy and I gave up our seats and spent the evening walking from room to room, pretending that we were sitting in the next room and merely visiting to see that everything was going well before returning to our seats.

Perhaps worst of all was an episode that occurred long ago, but that neither of us will ever forget. We had been married less than a year, and frankly I was overawed by my new in-laws. It was clear that they agreed Randy had married poorly, and they saw little reason to make the best of it. During those first years my mother-in-law seemed a formidable character but hardly in a class with Randy's Aunt Adele. Anyone who married into the family, including even Randy's mother, was considered by Adele to be an "adulteration." She managed to reduce me to wordless mutterings or to inanities. I don't believe that she was very tall, but she held herself erect with a kind of awful dignity, and her accent, acquired from heaven knows where, was positively royal English.

In the fall of 1932, in the depth of the Depression, we moved into our first home, a sublet in the elegant Volney Hotel on Seventy-fourth Street and Madison Avenue in New York. It consisted of a furnished bedroom, a living room, and a kitchen in a closet, but it came with maid service at the quite reasonable price (even for 1932) of one hundred dollars a month. Thanks to Clementine Paddleford, the food expert who wrote for the *Herald Tribune,* I began to experiment in the kitchen-closet, depending on the recipes in her weekly "Dollar Dinner for Four." Her column was a lifesaver for young brides, and it encouraged me to risk having guests for dinner, particularly since I was incapable of halving her recipes, and preparing the full quantity for only two people meant leftovers. (Randy tended to discourage leftovers; apparently from his point of view, or that of his palate, the first round of any dish that I prepared was more than sufficient.) It was at his instigation that I managed to summon the courage to invite his fearsome Aunt Adele for dinner.

To this day I have never found a rational explanation for what happened. Certainly, I knew which night she was expected. Certainly, being newly married, we had relatively few friends, and so it was not difficult to keep track of our social life. Nonetheless, on the fateful night in question we accepted an invitation to dinner at the home of one of the very few couples we knew. At seven o'clock, with our coats and hats on, we opened the door to leave and found standing there—you guessed it—Randy's Aunt Adele.

It is true that there are times when words fail and probably should. There was no way to explain our presence in coats and hats. It was quite clear that, unbelievably and recklessly, we had forgotten.

Our world did not, as might have been expected, come to an abrupt end. Life does continue, even after a major catastrophe. It was a long winter's chill, but we were actually able to convince Aunt

Adele to come for dinner sometime later, although, admittedly, it was a good deal later.

I learned one important lesson from this very painful episode. When there is no conceivable excuse, don't try to conceive one. Still, one catastrophe should certainly not discourage anyone from entertaining. After all, it can only get better. I grew to know, respect, and really like Randy's aunt on the second and more fortuitous coming.

I do remember one surprise guest appearance for which Randy has never quite forgiven me. In 1952, Marshall Field, Sr., became the president of the Child Welfare League of America, and the first meeting at which he presided took place in June in New York. During the afternoon someone realized that there were no plans to entertain our out-of-town members, a socially unacceptable oversight! We looked hopefully at our president, who promptly explained that his apartment was under dust cloths for the summer, and therefore unavailable. As vice-president, and with no other volunteers coming forward, I said that although our apartment was rather undersized and although a meeting later that afternoon would prevent me from being home until seven o'clock, I would call our obliging housekeeper and ask her to set out ice, drinks, cheese, and crackers for an informal reception at five-thirty. Mr. Field kindly agreed to act as the host.

In due course I went to my meeting, and Randy arrived home to find the apartment full of strangers, and a genial white-haired gentleman standing next to the front door, saying, "How do you do. My name is Marshall Field and won't you come in?" Randy started backing out the door, but having no place to go he changed his mind and announced somewhat hesitantly, "But I live here!" He joined the party and actually had a good time, which did not keep him from complaining bitterly later.

I recommend thinking through all aspects of a situation before embarking on any kind of entertainment, and that includes, if at all possible, sharing your plans with other occupants of your home.

It is not only last-minute arrangements that can create problems. Disposing of out-of-date invitations as well as old guest lists can prevent awkward situations. I once returned an invitation card that I found on my desk to a hostess who went crazy trying to figure out why I had accepted a dinner she wasn't giving. She finally called me to say that the dinner had taken place two years ago, and in fact we had been there.

Whatever the emergency, it is irrational to lose the investment already made in a party by allowing the entire evening or day to be ruined. If we seem agitated, we are aware that the guests must be feeling miserably uncomfortable.

And as for the couple who arrived a day early in tuxedo and gold lamé, we invited them in, cooked extra hamburgers, and sat with them at the kitchen table in our scruffy bathrobes. They did return the next evening, and although they told us that the formal party was lovely, they confessed later that "the first party was really the best."

Our ultimate conclusion is quite simply this: When facing the unexpected situation, or the unexpected guest, dissimulate as much as possible, but at all costs retain the posture of gracious hosts.

10

Entertainment

Toasts, Skits, and After-Dinner Games

At dinner we offer a toast
Apropos and, if possible, clever
But we're cautious at roasts not to roast
Hurt feelings are always a NEVER
And after? a quiz to be solved
Or a song or a skit or a poem
Which keeps them all deeply involved
Until it is time to go home.

A glorious meal may not be enough to insure a glorious party. Sometimes and for some groups it may be necessary to provide entertainment. This does not mean hiring a well-known professional singer or a three-piece band, but it does mean additional thought and planning.

The type of entertainment obviously depends on the proclivities of the group and the reason for the party, and it may range from one or more toasts at dinner to, yes, the professional singer and band. For special occasions guests may be asked to prepare toasts and/or skits to be presented respectively during and after dinner. If the party is in celebration of a birthday or anniversary, the entertainment is consonant with the theme.

I prefer the type of activity in which guests can participate, but I know that there is something soothing about sitting back and being entertained. Whatever you plan should not require so much work that it is an effort for you or your guests; nor should anything ever be asked of, or presented to, your guests that is in the least embarrassing.

Toasts

Toasts, offered during dinner, can make individual guests or the hosts themselves feel wonderful. Most guests tend to believe and therefore are enchanted by a graceful compliment and the good wishes implicit in *santé, prosit, skaal,* and *shalom.* It seems significant to me that almost every language includes a word that signifies health, peace, and well-being. Toasts are a form of entertainment and a way of saying welcome to guests and thank you to hosts.

We have a friend who has the faculty of going around a table, toasting each guest, and saying something both charming and appropriate about each in turn. Everyone loves it, but I am inclined to believe multiple toasts of this type should be undertaken only by people with memories and self-confidence. I have a good deal of confidence, but there are times when I have suddenly and irretrievably lost the name of a friend and guest just as I have risen to propose a toast.

One toast, or series of toasts, I will never forget was delivered at a friend's home by Mary Lindsay, former Mayor John Lindsay's charming wife, who at that time I knew only slightly. The party was in honor of Mary's birthday, and in imitation of her hostess, the guest of honor started toasting friends around the table. Actually everyone there, except Randy and me, was a close friend. We had been invited in the same way that I have occasionally asked someone inappropriate because I happened to see them.

On this particular evening, Mary started by saying something like, "And Joan, my dear friend who was in college with me and has gone on to become the distinguished director of—" and "Harry, our very special longtime friend, who is such a great leader—." Reaching me, she looked startled for a moment, and then said rather dramatically, "And Elly! What can I say about Elly?" after which she proceeded to the next guest.

Toasts are traditionally proposed during dinner, but they certainly need not include all the guests at the table. They offer a way of saying something pleasant, and since almost everyone loves the sound of his or her name and a minute or two in the spotlight, they need not be clever to be successful. The host and/or hostess may begin by toasting the guest of honor, or all and any of the other guests. Those seated next to the hosts may offer toasts in gratitude to the hospitality and charm of the evening. And very talented hosts like my friend may choose to drink to the health of each guest seriatim, with an appropriate compliment.

Skits, Songs, and Poems

Skits, satirical songs, and poems are fun to do and to hear. They are usually offered after dinner, and in connection with a birthday or anniversary or some other special occasion. People enjoy them even if the iambuses are not exactly pentameter. If the performer is clever, a good speaker, a poet, *and* funny, so much the better. If not, it is still worthwhile, and with a little practice most of us find that eventually we can develop the necessary skills in order to be poetic and even funny.

Most of us, from time to time, have received invitations that suggest we should bring a poem or skit in honor of a birthday or anniversary. Obviously the form of the suggestion should make it clear that this is purely voluntary. For some people the idea of performing, even in front of close friends, can be traumatic. Fortunately it isn't really difficult to write a poem or put words to a song.

In today's lyrical world no one expects to be strictly confined by meter or rhyme. If you are musically inclined you may want to write an original song. If not, there are a good many multi-syllabic songs that allow a large number of words to be included in each line, so that you won't need to worry about a rhyme scheme after every four or five words. Select something simple, like the "Battle Hymn of the Republic" (seven metric feet) or "Yankee Doodle Dandy."

If you have trouble with simple songs like the above, I suggest that you adjust the music to suit your needs or go to straight poetry. You might try emulating Ogden Nash and say whatever you want, ignoring rhythm and putting a rhyme in when it suits you; for example, "We have gathered here tonight to pay special tribute to Joe / whom we all know / and whom we have always admired / even though his golf game leaves a great deal to be desired," and so forth. You won't win any laurel wreaths, but Joe will be pleased.

If you want to attempt a more structured effort, make your life easy by ending each line with a word for which there are a large number of rhymes. Words ending with *-ate* are a good example: "We've gathered to congratulate / a man whom we would like to state / is someone, if we chose to rate / on looks or style or any trait / or as a brother, friend, or mate / could get us all to stay up late / to chat or just to cogitate / the reason is that chance, or fate / has made him so articulate / that we agree he's simply great." Get it? For other easy rhyme schemes use *-en* (men, ten, when, den, hen, then) or *-ane* (main, lane, sane, vain, wane, gain) or *-ood* (mood, crude, dude, food, lewd, imbued, allude) Avoid words ending with *-oof*. After you have said, "Dear friend I'd like to offer proof / although your dog may act aloof / his doghouse needs a shingled roof / another type would be a goof / and that might make him murmur "woof," the rhymes are limited in number, and besides they are not conducive to wishing anyone a happy birthday, with the exception of your dog. With *-ate,* you at least have *celebrate* and *congratulate* to work with.

Some poems work better if you skip a rhyme. As an example, I can offer a song set to the tune of "Reuben, Reuben" in honor of a gentleman who is a highly successful entrepreneur in the fertilizer business. He has always prided himself on the high social status of his clients, which include members of the Dupont family and a number of prominent owners of estates in Newport. One of the verses went as follows: "Doesn't cater to the masses / Up in Newport he's a hit / Mingles with the upper classes / They use Uncle Jerry's products."

Even in the old-fashioned, structured rhyme scheme there is room for variation.

If you have no idea what to write about, try stringing together the names of guests who are attending the party:

> *Hey there, Lucy, here we are*
> *All your friends from near and far*
> *Since you were a blushing bride*
> *Good lord, how we have multiplied.*
> *Fisher, Frank and Cahn and Low*
> *Gathered here to say hello*
> *Hyatt, Tully, Walker, Bright*
> *Everyone is here tonight*
> *Ehrman, Block, and both the Franks*
> *Here to swell the happy ranks."*

See? It's easier than you thought. No matter how corny it is, people love amateur hours, and that lovely musical sound of their own names. You really don't have to worry about being funny. No one expects it. The guest or couple being honored by your effort will be grateful; the other guests will be too worried about their performances to hear yours.

On one of my birthdays my youngest son substituted a mass poetic effort for the usual toast. He distributed a single line to each group of three guests and instructed them to add a rhyming line. After a few minutes the couplets were combined and the resulting full poem was read. I don't recall the exact words, but I believe they were somewhat close to the following:

Happy birthday and a whole lot more
Though you're not as youthful as before
You look only thirty-nine to us
Thirty-nine and just a little plus
Friends that you've collected may be many
And this party cost a pretty penny
May your life be beautiful and warm
Just as long as Randy can perform
Still we're very glad that we are here
Have a happy birthday, Elly dear.

Pretty weak, but as my son remarked, too many poets are liable to make any poem verse.

Active Postdinner Activities

The enthusiasm for games that require activity on the part of the guests seems to have waned considerably. Such activities of my youth as spin-the-bottle would be considered absurd by most young people today, although at one time it was quite risqué. Still, there are some forms of active after-dinner entertainment that have survived. They include games like charades; similar games copied from television, such as Win, Lose, and Draw; card games such as bridge, canasta, and poker; and board games, including backgammon, played for stakes low enough to make losing unimportant, of course. There are also a large number of games that test intelligence, which should be used only if the particular guests enjoy having their intelligence tested.

Certain games have surfaced briefly, become obsessions, and then faded away. At one time we played Chinese Checkers regularly, and subsequently we became immersed, nightly, in Scrabble. My grandchildren beat me consistently at Trivia for a period of two years. I was delighted when the Trivia cards joined Simon (Says) at the top of the closet.

For certain guests, at a certain time dancing to tapes or records or discs (whatever the current state of the art prescribes) is fun. Far more usual are the more passive forms of entertainment that allow guests to be entertained without making any effort.

Sit and Relax

My mother-in-law provided musical entertainment for guests after dinner, partly because she enjoyed music and partly because, during the Depression years, there were so many musicians who needed work. She would arrange small chairs in the living room for musicales where the stiffly collared gentlemen would perch uncomfortably for an hour of Bach or Haydn. I remember that when I went to her home for the first time, she mentioned that she was having a quartet to entertain her guests that evening. "But you have six chairs for the performers!" I said. "This quartet has six musicians," she responded firmly. I learned subsequently that quartets at my mother-in-law's home ranged from three to eight, with four the least likely number.

Some of my friends still offer live music as entertainment after dinner, but that has become rare. In fact, most forms of after-dinner entertainment seem to be disappearing, except for special occasions, such as birthdays and stag parties. We used to have a fortune teller once in a while, but that can be dangerous unless you provide advance information and you can trust the seer to see only healthy and wealthy futures. With that assurance, a fortune teller is a fortuitous choice as entertainment.

I remember a particular evening when my mother had a graphologist who was considered a great expert and who amused her guests by analyzing their characters as demonstrated by their penmanship. She enchanted a lady who was known for miserliness by explaining that her writing revealed one major fault, excessive generosity.

Entertainers, from musicians to gorillas, are available for postdinner entertainment. In one case, a friend of ours arranged to have a gorilla with balloons and original messages for her husband's birthday. Unfortunately, the gentleman encased in the gorilla suit arrived in a late stage of inebriation, and it was almost necessary to summon the police. Obviously, this type of situation should be avoided, which suggests that careful investigation should precede the hiring of enter-tainers.

After a good many observations as well as personal experiences, some successful and some verging on disaster, we have concluded that there is no substitute for good conversation. As part of a genera-tion addicted to television and therefore constantly exposed to pas-sive entertainment, we now agree that if it is possible to include guests with special knowledge or special perspectives at a dinner; intelligent discussions are the best entertainment of all.

11

Aftermath

Cleaning Up the Debris

Though the food was delicious
We're not in the mood
To face dirty dishes
And leftover food
What spoils or what melts
Has been hidden from view
And for everything else?
Well, tomorrow will do.

D inner is over, and the guests are still discussing various fascinating topics in their respective groups. With everyone happily involved, we begin to think about cleaning up. If we have used a caterer, or if we have helpers who can be trusted to remove and store, we continue hosting. If not, there are some chores that demand immediate attention.

When I have been the cook and bottle washer, with only amateur assistants, I follow a carefully devised plan. At the conclusion of the meal, and as soon as I can safely leave the guests to their own devices, or to Randy, I clear the table of leftover food and store anything that requires refrigeration. Next, I make sure that used dishes, glassware, and flatware are inconspicuous. At that point I rejoin my guests and leave any heavier work for later, and when Randy can help me; not until after the guests have gone does the scraping and reordering of the kitchen take place. And not until the next day do we restore our home to its pristine preparty condition.

Whether the cleanup process involves a good deal of effort or very little, anything that must be done before the guests have said their last good nights should attract as little attention as possible. The prolonged absence of the hosts, accompanied by the splash of running water, the clinking of glassware, and the thudding sound of the opening and closing of cupboard doors in the kitchen has a deadening effect on conversation in the living room and may even attract guilty volunteers whose efforts one would gladly avoid. Besides, one should help guests to leave feeling that the magic is still there and that a genie will appear from nowhere and sweep everything back into place.

The only step that must be taken at the risk of deserting guests briefly is the refrigeration of leftovers. Particularly such items as meat, fish, poultry, and sauces made with uncooked eggs require cooling while they still have the bloom of youth. Heating them to a temperature of one hundred and seventy degrees or more may take care of any unfriendly bacteria, but it will not restore flavor that has been lost during an extended period in a warm room.

Of course, the storing of leftover food presupposes that it will be served again in a timely fashion, and that means no more than a day or, at the most, two. (When there is room in a freezer and the item has not spent time there before the party, the holding period can be extended.) However, if you are planning to leave on a vacation the day after the party, you should probably offer one of your guests a doggy bag.

When attention to guests, which always takes precedence, makes it impossible to spend even a few moments on this first phase of cleanup, and when, therefore, food has been unrefrigerated for an extended period of time, I recommend the garbage pail or disposal as a final resting place.

After the spoils of the evening have been stowed or thrown away, plates and silverware may still need to be removed or made invisible. Guests who are settling in for a pleasant conversation should not be exposed to a view of potable or comestible remainders. Glasses that are half full (or half empty, depending on your philosophy) are not attractive decorations resting in a living room, and neither are plates with the remnants of food. You might try draping a large cloth over the dining table until you have time to clear everything away later, thus concealing the plates and silverware from the vision of the guests; or with some help, the table can be cleared immediately, and dishes piled on shelves and counters in the kitchen until they can be scraped, washed, and stored.

Although I do not consider paper plates and cups suitable for most parties, I do use them occasionally for family events, and I always have a large box or similar container available so that I can dispose of all the plates and cups simply and rapidly. At all other times, when I use our regular china and glassware, I make sure that there is uncluttered space in the kitchen, so that they can be piled up until the guests have gone, at which time they can be moved to a dishwasher.

It is better not to attempt the scraping, rinsing, and transferring to a dishwasher until you have time to do this carefully, and with less risk of breakage. After one party for some corporate types, including several bankers, we were in a hurry to clean up as quickly as possible, since some of them had expressed a desire to see our newly renovated kitchen. As a result, a fork from our best sterling set was lost in the garbage, and we were left with what Randy refers to as a "banker's dozen," two less than the proverbial baker's thirteen. To avoid a similar unfortunate occurrence, I now suggest to any helpers that they count the silverware at the conclusion of a party, to be sure that nothing has been thrown away inadvertently, and I repeat the counting process the next day before the garbage truck has permanently transported a sterling-silver fork to oblivion.

Leaving dirty dishes lying around overnight is an invitation to various unwelcome creatures, but the final stages of cleaning up can well be left until the next day. Nothing will happen to chairs or tables that are out of place or to the paper guest-towels in the bathroom wastebasket, and of course it is more fun to go to bed while we are still somewhat fresh and still caught up in the exhilaration of a happy event, than with a feeling of exhaustion.

It isn't easy to make the cleaning-up phase of entertaining sound jolly, but it doesn't have to be arduous if it is done in an organized and leisurely fashion; and if you have the right kind of help, and I don't mean professional assistance, it really can be fun. This is one area that Randy avoids, for which I am grateful. He has convinced me (and I do not doubt that this is by design) that he is hopelessly clumsy and that I can count on at least one good irreplaceable item broken if I allow him to take part in handling soapy dishes.

I have one friend who may stay a little later and help when she has been a guest. But the best solution, at least for me, has been a friend who comes over the next day for coffee, leftover cake, cleanup, and gossip. Restoring the house while reviewing the party, and particularly the shortcomings of some of the guests, makes short work, indeed, of even the lengthiest of household chores.

12

Curtain Calls

Time to Retire

We try not to yawn
For that wouldn't be right!
But it's getting toward dawn.
Won't you please say good night?

During the first year of our marriage, the love and honor almost disintegrated as a result of some inconsiderate guests, and my untrained husband. We had invited a couple whom we knew slightly and who were socially very important, or at least so they implied. I went to inordinate trouble over dinner, a good part of which was prepared by my mother's cook. But just the business of setting the table and organizing the service of the main course was exhausting.

The evening was a great success, up to a point. By midnight the important couple had shown no inclination toward leaving. Despite growing fatigue, I continued to behave as a model hostess. Randy, on the other hand, had disappeared at about 11:45, and his absence had become embarrassing. I opened the bedroom door to call him from the bathroom, where I assumed he had gone and may have lost track of time while reading. There, quite visible to the guests, was Randy, curled up in bed in his pajamas. Our subsequent discussion was a good deal warmer than the atmosphere surrounding the guests' departure. Our marriage survived just barely, but our friendship with the socially prominent couple did not.

For every party, depending on the type of event and the customs of a particular social group, there comes a time when guests reasonably may be expected to leave. That time will differ in accordance with the day of the week, the geographic area, and the average age of the guests. For instance, in suburban areas it is probably understood that parties held between Monday and Friday will break up early enough to allow guests to drive home soberly, have a reasonable night's sleep, and thus arrive at the train station in the morning with at least one eye open. On the other hand, the curfew may be quite extended on Friday and Saturday nights. Parties in the city on an average may start and end somewhat later.

Our friends are no longer young executives working on an upwardly mobile track that requires them to put in one hundred and twenty hours a week at the office. Still, although their work hours are shorter, their sleep requirements have increased. We consider eleven o'clock the time by which farewells should be completed, except for charitable functions in hotels, which should not extend beyond ten o'clock, and balls for ninetieth birthdays, which may end as late as midnight if the guest of honor doesn't end before that. The young and middle-aged party goers tend to limit their social activities to weekends, in which case the curfew may be flexible.

It is not necessary to remain as long at an event that starts at 6:30 as at one scheduled to begin at 7:45. Of course, it is considered good manners to wait until dessert and coffee have been served before saying good night, although even that rule can be breached if the service of dinner has been unduly extended. There is no commandment that requires a guest to risk a sleepless night or a next-day headache for the sake of hosts who have failed to organize a reasonably timed party. However, this does not mean that a guest should become famous, or infamous, for always being the first to leave a party, unless he or she is willing to forfeit future invitations.

Lingerers

Hosts may be flattered if a party continues beyond the usual hour, but even highly successful parties should be finite. Most couples who have been hosts for a significant number of years have developed a system of eye signals by which they communicate information. Randy and I believe that our signals are imperceptible, but at the moment that I say to him—silently of course—"Are these people ever going home?" and he responds, equally silently, "I hope to God, but I'm beginning to doubt it!" someone senses the secret communication and has the good sense to yawn, stand up, and begin the process of saying good night.

For hosts who have played their role diligently during an entire evening, and who are quite ready to call it a day, or a night, there is nothing as depressing as the marathon valedictory. Everyone has gathered at the door, prepared to depart, when the raconteur of the group, and there is usually a raconteur in every group, suddenly recalls something immensely unimportant that cannot wait for another date.

One friend of ours has devised a way to speed the parting guest. Some years ago he bought a broken-down sofa for $2.50 at a junk shop, which was subsequently rebuilt and recovered for $250. In its finished form it represented an incredible bargain; covered in charming chintz, it looked quite handsome, but it was also the most uncomfortable piece of furniture imaginable. Over a period of time he noticed that guests who sat there either moved or went home immediately. Now, when a guest outstays his welcome, our friend says, "Do bring your drink over and sit here with me. I want to talk to you." He swears that the effect is miraculous. Within no more than ten minutes, the guest is aware of the lateness of the hour and the exodus begins.

I do not recommend this method, since it violates my own principles of hospitality. Nevertheless, we do stop serving drinks at an appropriately late hour, and we allow the conversational levels to subside a bit. Both of these ploys encourage departure.

Spoil Sports

The other side of the late-departing or long-lingering guest problem is the disruption created by the couple who breaks up the party at ten o'clock, when I have every reason to hope that it will last another hour. Even if everyone is having a marvelous time, the early departure of just one or more guests can set off a lemming reaction; everyone stands up simultaneously and heads upstream.

There is grace in leaving at the right time, neither too early nor too late, and good manners require making the departure sweet, but short. That caveat includes the hosts, who should refrain from begging guests to "stay a little while longer."

Anything that needs saying by hosts as well as guests can probably be said on the phone the next day. A thank-you can be enlarged upon in a note. Single gentlemen who do not intend to reciprocate may send flowers on the following day—if they have not sent them on the day of the party, which is far more desirable. Next-day flowers are often a nuisance. We are probably either going out for dinner on the day after a party or planning on eating leftovers in the kitchen. Besides, I will have to write a thank-you note to acknowledge the flowers, when I could easily have expressed gratitude personally on the previous night. On the other hand, guests who send arrangements or plants on the day of the party, and who are wise enough to select blossoms that will not conflict with the colors of our living room and that do not require an effort to fix, are always invited again.

13

Children's Hour

Parties for the Twenty-first–Century Crowd

*May heaven give us all the power
To live through one more children's hour.*

E ven parents who have overcome any hesitancy about giving parties for their adult friends may turn pale at the thought of having their seven-year-old son's class for a birthday celebration. Children's parties are often a delicate balancing act: In order to find favor in your child's eyes, originality may be necessary, while at the same time there must be conformance with practices instituted by the parents of his or her friends.

Because I have worked in child-care organizations for a large part of my life, I understand how important parties are to children. They do, or should, provide a period of happiness in a world that many children find grim and frightening, and they can be valuable learning experiences. Children need to develop socialization skills. The enhancement of friendship, the encouragement of communication, and the building of confidence are all educational products of a successful children's party.

The fear of losing control of a party has some validity when the affair is for seven-year-olds. On one long ago but still vivid occasion, I left eleven second-grade friends of my youngest son, whom I was about to escort to see the Rockettes at Radio City, while I went to the bedroom for a hat and a pocketbook. I returned to find a dozen squalling, squirming, navy-blue-suited young gentlemen happily beating each other vigorously. I should report that I was able to regain control, but only after there had been some damage: a bloody nose and a torn jacket sleeve, both of which were repaired in time to take in the Rockettes.

Police duty aside, children's parties are not too different from adult events. Both require planning, appropriate food and service, and a sense of gracious hospitality. For children at the youngest age levels, this implies helping them not only to share toys but to appear willing to do so (although it's important to accept the fact that achieving this may be impossible). Humor, a relaxed attitude, and a clear sense of pleasure on the part of parents in the guests and the birthday child are more important than the presence of a highly paid magician or clown. A recent party for a group of two-year-olds underscored this for me. The clown was handsomely made-up, imposing, and very expensive. At least half the children greeted his efforts at joviality with screams and tears.

Some of the working mothers and fathers I know worry constantly about the time spent away from home, the child-care arrangements they have made, and their need to spend quality time with their offspring. This guilt has been compounded by the reports issued by experts on child development, early education, and bonding. To compensate for what they perceive as their own parental shortcomings, these families may spend far too much money on a party, and become irritable when their child seems ungrateful. Expense and a party that is fun for children are unrelated. Extravagance is never necessary, and certainly for very young children it is not even in good taste.

The Diaper Set

Parties on first and second birthdays are usually celebrations for parents and relatives. Infants in high chairs may feel some degree of self-importance, but they are more likely to be feeling the ice cream and cake with both hands. By the second birthday, children will sense an aura of excitement and may even enjoy a party that is not overprogrammed. With two or three children, each of whom will play alone rather than with each other, and with understanding parents who can accept that two-year-olds have not reached the stage of being generous or hospitable, the birthday event can be satisfactory.

By the third birthday, children begin to act as hosts, with, of course, lots of parental guidance. A number of restaurants offer totally packaged parties, thus relieving parents of all the details, but I believe that home parties are less tiring for children and therefore more liable to prevent the postparty tears.

Elementary-School Years

When children reach school age a little more structure is in order, with due appreciation of the value of free expression. A number of the most successful parties that I remember from my own childhood, and that of my children, were simple picnics in a park or in the country. My birthday coincided with strawberry time. In several different years my friends and I went picking strawberries, using the baskets that had contained our picnic lunch. Prizes were awarded to those with the fullest baskets at the end of no more than forty-five minutes of picking, or as soon as my mother judged that interest was lagging. I never won a prize, because I always ate more than half of what I picked before the baskets were judged. I like to believe I was being a gracious hostess, although my mother never gave me credit for this.

Complicated parties are always less successful. I recall a late-summer afternoon at our rented country house, when we had taken my son and his friends to an amusement park for carousel rides. I had indulged in a novel idea—novel, at least, to this particular age group. After the carousel rides we returned to the house, where I had hidden small gifts in bushes. After the children had searched in vain for the promised "treasures," I went to look and discovered that the packages had all disappeared. Apparently moving men who had come in our absence to pick up boxes to take to New York, had spotted the packages and, for some never-explained reason, had loaded them on their truck for transportation to the city. Fifteen disappointed five-year-olds went home empty-handed, and I was left to face my son's disapproval. I determined to keep future parties as simple as possible and to encourage my sons to take an active part in planning their activities.

Preteens

As children get to the boy-girl stage, and that may be as early as twelve or even eleven, dancing to records or tapes at home is fun, but there are a good many other ways to entertain young people. Take over two tennis courts at a club or in the park and run a round-robin tournament; have a swimming party; take a group to a local hockey, basketball, or baseball game and arrange for birthday greetings to be posted on the scoreboard during halftime (many stadium managers are happy to provide this amenity); organize a softball or touch-football game; if you have a large-screen TV set, rent a cassette and pass the popcorn; or rent a camcorder and provide the script for a home movie in which all the guests can participate.

Sometime after my twelfth birthday I became interested in boys, and particularly in one older man of fourteen. That was the winter when my friends and I started dancing school at a certain Miss O'Neil's studio. The boys all wore navy-blue suits and white shirts with stiffly starched collars. They were also required to wear white cotton gloves to ensure that no grubby paw prints would blemish our pastel taffeta dresses. It was Miss O'Neil's responsibility to instruct us not only in how to one-two-slide but in acceptable social behavior. Our first formal introduction to the opposite sex and the attitudes we were expected to adopt toward each other were carefully composed in the mirrored ballroom of Miss O'Neil's laboratory.

Graduating from dancing school, we were still not ready for the large stage. The girls' parents arranged small dances at home, which the boys' parents ordered them to attend. We required a victrola that had to be wound between, and sometimes in the middle of, each record, and we danced the charleston to "Sweet Georgia Brown," and "Tiger Rag."

The Late Teens

Parties were the most important part of life for the older teenagers of the 1920s. Some of the enchantment of the parties for the privileged young in the early part of the century did prepare a path to courtship, marriage, and life. We even emerged with social consciences, and we became the goo-goos of the 1930s. For those who were born much later, "goo-goo" derived from "good government," which translated into liberalism. The party world I grew up in apparently didn't stultify the ability of our generation to take life, and social problems, seriously.

It seems strange to compare today's customs with those of my youth. There was much that was wrong and artificial in the attitudes of our parents, way back in the years when I was a girl. Some of the snobbishness of that era was deplorable, and the attitudes toward sex were not designed to help young people in their passage to maturity. Still, we did learn social customs and deportment, and we had an opportunity to begin the process of "getting to know you" with members of the opposite sex. The postscripts to Miss O'Neil's ballroom were the balls given by our parents in the great ballrooms of the major hotels. As a marriage mart, these dances were effective. They brought together the young people whom our respective families considered suitable; and as proof positive of the success of the system, I met Randy at his cousin's ball in 1929.

When I look back to the birthday parties that punctuated my childhood and adolescent years, it is always with a kind of glow. Being the center of attention, surrounded by friends, all of whom wanted to sit next to me on this special day, and looking at the happy faces of my parents were all part of the wonder of being a year older. Presents were important, but even more important was the aura of approval. Parents so rarely take the time to truly see their children! Children's parties make an essential contribution not only to child development but to parent-child relationships, assuming that a few simple rules, many of which apply to all ages including octogenarian, are observed:

1. **Be Conscious of Time.** Exhausted children quickly become unhappy, and no party should result in unhappy children. Parties for any age group should be time-organized so that they will begin and end within rational limits.

2. **Keep it Simple,** or at least sufficiently uncomplicated so that the resources and the good humor of the hosts are not strained. Too many activities, too much food, too accelerated a pace ensures a memorable party, and the memories are all liable to be bad.

3. **Select the Right Environment.** A party held in a living room with rare bibelots on the tables is an invitation to disaster. My godchild, age sixteen months, came with her family for a festive dinner last year. As might have been expected for a child of that age, she escaped our watchful eyes and in one moment overturned

a table and broke a Chinese-export saucer. Child- or party-proofing a home is wise if you want to protect irreplaceable treasures. (Remember, however, that even less replaceable than porcelain are the good feelings of guests. Hospitality demands a smile, even as your best lamp comes crashing to the floor.)

4. Avoid Imprisonment! Having to sit for an extended period of time is a form of imprisonment, even if the entertainment is expensive. Being involved in some way in an activity is good for children of all ages.

5. Adapt Entertainment or Activities to Age and to the Proclivities of the Group. For some children and their friends, competitive games are desirable. Potato races and pin-the-tail-on-the-donkey are classic and still popular with the preschool groups. Aerobic classes or swimming at the neighborhood "Y" may be the choice of an older group, and dancing to records at home is always fun for teenagers.

When the guests have gone, when the magic disappears, the birthday child's letdown is often accompanied by tears. These are not really a symbol of unhappiness, but rather a tribute to a day that has been successful and just a little overexciting.

14

Surprise, Surprise

To Do or Not to Do

A surprise may be fun, but you should be admonished
It's often the hosts who are really astonished.

Some dear friends gave a surprise cocktail reception for Randy and me on our twentieth anniversary. Another friend had volunteered to get me there, with a story that I swallowed rather easily. She explained that a number of large philanthropic foundations were having a reception, and that she had been told she could bring me. As a chronic wooer of foundations for one cause or another, I was delighted by the invitation and grateful to the friend who had arranged it.

Because it's never wise to look affluent when appealing for funds. I arrived in my oldest suit, and totally uncoiffed. To make matters worse, when we got to the party I looked around, saw a number of close friends, and said lugubriously, "Where are the foundations?" an unfortunate remark with which the hosts were not too pleased. Randy, on the other hand, simply refused to come, so the friend deputized to convince him finally gave up in despair and resorted to the practical device of saying, "Dammit! They're giving you a surprise party and I'm supposed to get you there so will you damn well stop making it so difficult?"

Surprise parties can be exciting, and great fun for those who give them. There is some question, however, whether they are as much fun for the recipient of the surprise. More often than not the person who is to be surprised gets wind of it in advance and therefore suffers from anticipatory trauma. There is some justification in worrying how to fake total astonishment even though you are wearing your best clothes and have obviously just left the hairdresser. Under those circumstances, astonishment can require Oscar-level acting, which, for most amateurs, is close to impossible. For the few of us who are so dense that we suspect nothing, the surprise may be so complete that we may make an inadvertent remark, for which we will have to apologize for years afterward.

One surprise party I will never forget was given by my mother on a birthday some years after my marriage. Mother had not realized the changes that had taken place in our list of friends. Many of those whom I had known earlier had drifted away, and Randy and I had made new and closer friends of couples whom we had met in the last few years. Some of the guests Mother invited we had not seen in five or more years, and they were probably as surprised by the invitation as I was to see them. Other friends who were not invited were decidedly cool to us afterward.

If, despite the potential for disaster, you are still intent on giving a surprise party, it may be heartening to know that most of your guests, with the possible exception of the honoree, will have a wonderful time. There is nothing to compare to the excitement of those moments when everyone is standing in a darkened room while the lookout reports, "Ssh! They're coming." The guests are sharing an important moment, and they are bound together by the experience. The hubbub that ensues is an enormous party plus: "Surprise!" "Were you really surprised?" "I'll bet you suspected!" "I think it really was a surprise! Did you see how pale he looked?" (Extreme pallor is the litmus test of a successful surprise, and impossible to fake.)

Of course the first step in planning a surprise party is making sure of the date. If the ones to be surprised have secretly arranged to be trekking in the Himalayas on the date of their anniversary, it will undoubtedly be the hosts who are surprised. Next, careful planning is necessary to ensure that even if they are not trekking in the Himalayas, they will somehow appear at the proper time and place, totally unprepared for a party but suitably dressed for one.

This last takes ingenuity. Sometimes a member of the family arranges a small dinner that turns out to be a large one. If it is a spouse or live-in who is to be surprised, it is essential that he or she be kept from arriving home before the guests are assembled. I managed that once by telling Randy that I had forgotten something and that we needed to return home before meeting a couple at a restaurant. When he unlocked the front door, he saw twenty of his friends holding drinks, at which point he said, indignantly, "What the hell are you doing here?"

If there *is* a question about possible adverse reactions, the best solution is to drop a hint or two. The guests at the party will still have a wonderful time, and the guest-of-honor will not have to do penance afterward for an untoward remark.

We recently received an invitation that had, in red letters on the outside, the word "Sssh!!" The rest of the information was on the inside: a party for a sixtieth birthday; no answers by mail, please, or by phone unless it was to regret (to avoid a rash of phone calls, which might alert the birthday boy). Also, we were asked to refrain from mentioning the party to anyone, simply to avoid any discussion that might be overheard. With such precautions in place there was a good chance that the party would be a surprise; and, besides, the honoree-to-be had made it so abundantly clear to his wife that the *last thing on earth he wanted was a surprise party* that he had little reason for suspicion.

The birthday boy had been told he was going to celebrate a friend's anniversary with two other couples. At the last moment the plans had been changed, and the lunch had been transferred to a country club. When he arrived, sixty guests were waiting for him and all of them were thrilled by the extent of his surprise. He didn't lapse into a coma, although that might have been the ultimate compliment to his wife's ingenuity, but he did turn pale and then red in succession. What's more, he later admitted that he loved the party, which was tailored to his tastes: a lunch of mountainous portions of pasta followed by a golf putting contest. Apparently he had overestimated his aversion to being surprised.

In addition to deciding how you will get the guest of honor to the right place, on time, and in the proper state of astonishment and dress, you should include with the invitation strict and precise instructions about maintaining secrecy. Phoning may be the safest way to ensure that guests actually understand they should not mention the party and that they should be discreet about sending presents. A gift from someone who has never known the date of your birth is a dead giveaway. If you send written invitations, you may wish to indicate "no gifts," and it should certainly be made clear, in large letters, that the party is to be a surprise. You might also suggest that they call you at your office with questions or with their responses and that they avoid calling your home at all.

I have now painted both sides of the canvas, and you will have to decide for yourself whether a surprise party for someone who is celebrating a special birthday or anniversary is worth the trouble and the risk. Will it be a brilliant success for everyone, or will the particular person you are planning to surprise be totally miserable? On balance, perhaps it doesn't matter too much, since the rest of the company will have such a lovely time. Sssssh!

15

Odd Hours

From Breakfast to After-Theater Dining

Canapés, snacks or small cakes on a tray
Parties are fun any time of the day
Scones and preserves, pastry, kaffee mit Schlag
Eat like a bird or indulge like a hog
Omelette, a quiche, and a pancake or crêpe
Then off to a "fat farm" for back into shape.

T he company of friends can be a pleasure at any time of the day or night, with the possible exception of the hours between midnight and 7:00 A.M.; and even those wee hours may be suitable if your friends are nightingales. For the rest of us, more conventional times are appropriate, and that means not only planning around regular meal hours, but thinking of odd hours such as 11:00 in the morning for coffee and danish, mid-afternoon for tea and crumpets, and 10:30 to midnight for posttheater or concert suppers. Timing should be adjusted to your friends' preferences and to your schedule and theirs.

It may be easier to assemble the group you want to entertain at a Sunday brunch, or even a weekday breakfast, than at a dinner. I find that my fast-track grandchildren, whose workdays end at ten or later in the evening, may accept an invitation to a family gathering over pancakes on a Sunday morning, while dinner at eight is out of the question. I do not recall my mother having guests for breakfast parties; nor was the word "brunch" part of her vocabulary. I do remember luncheons, which were almost as formal as dinners, and occasionally mother served tea, coffee, finger sandwiches, and cookies at four in the afternoon, presiding behind a handsome sterling-silver service.

We have a number of single friends who welcome an invitation to a party on Sundays when the day may seem long and lonely. Besides our single friends we know a growing number of women (many of them former "ladies who lunch") whose business schedules are heavier than those of most men. Now if I want to see them I accommodate my party schedule to their executive calendar, and that may mean breakfast with juice and bran muffins during the week, or brunch on the weekend.

Seven to Ten in the Morning

Breakfast is a pleasant and often convenient time to entertain. Breakfast menus range from coffee and Danish for weekday meetings of committees, or a weekend breakfast of fruit and oat bran followed by aerobics for some of my women friends who are health nuts, to waffles, eggs, bacon, and sausages for breakfast enthusiasts like me. There is no other meal that requires more adaptation to the tastes and eccentricities of the guests. Breakfast is highly personal and for most people does not allow for deviation from a daily program. We have one friend who must start the day with cranberry juice, bran, and a special, esoteric brand of herbal tea. Fortunately she brings her own tea with her when she comes for breakfast.

When the breakfast is for a large group I try to offer a variety of dishes, so that everyone will find their accustomed fare. The basic menu always includes some form of the time-honored American traditional bacon and eggs, and I do have some individual packages of cold cereal and skimmed milk for the cholesterol conscious.

A few years ago, when New York was celebrating a Salute to Great Britain, I gave a breakfast for some of the British women who were visiting. I knew that breakfasts in England were hearty, and although I did not offer kippers, our menu was designed to assuage hunger for at least an hour or two. We had an "omelette man" stationed at a table in the dining room, who offered a choice of fillings: fines herbes, bacon, mushrooms, cheese, or all four. Sides of smoked salmon, breads and muffins, strawberries and crème fraîche, and coffee completed the menu. Actually our British guests were well fed, since they attended two breakfasts that morning. "Breakfast at Tiffany" was more glamorous than our party, but the tactful guests said that they preferred the intimacy and the food at our home. Pleasant to hear, even if they made similar remarks to the president of Tiffany!

At the average breakfast party it is hardly necessary to have omelettes, or to hire anyone as expensive as a professional omelette chef. In fact, it is easier and less expensive to entertain at breakfast than at any other time, although bear in mind that you may get correspondingly less credit from those whose past hospitality you are repaying.

Eleven in the Morning to Two-thirty

Brunch is an elaboration of breakfast. Eggs Benedict, oeufs en gelée, crêpes with assorted fillings, or even waffles with creamed chicken are all suitable. I went through a horrendous period of entertaining at brunch after having acquired a waffle iron. During the entire meal I sat in a corner turning out waffles and ladling creamed chicken. My friends assured me that the meal was delicious, but I wouldn't know; I was always too busy making waffles.

I rarely give luncheons except in celebration of birthdays, since most of my friends are on diets and saving their calories for dinner. On the few occasions when I do give a party in the middle of the day, it's on a Saturday for my working friends, and a weekday for my older, long-since-retired chums. At the formal seated luncheon for this latter category, I use my best table mats and an extravagant floral centerpiece. At luncheons for women the menu consists of food that is pretty: perhaps chicken or crabmeat salad, decorated with sun-dried tomatoes, radicchio, and watercress, and accompanied by tiny sandwiches; or lamb chops and French beans with a light dessert or a soufflé. Whatever I serve, the platters must be art forms.

I am more nervous about the details of a luncheon for my older female friends that I am giving a dinner in honor of the governor of Minnesota. With less on their minds, I find retired ladies enjoy picking apart not just the chicken salad but the hostess as well.

Four to Six in the Afternoon

Tea has always seemed to me the most civilized of meals. I still remember with much pleasure the teas at Mrs. Vincent Astor's (the first Mrs. Astor) at her home at 130 East Eightieth Street, where the Philharmonic auxiliary board met once a month. My mother-in-law, who ran a good many of the musical organizations in New York and who eventually forgave me for marrying Randy, had involved me in the Philharmonic Junior Committee. After the meetings, at which the discussion sometimes centered on the value of graduating from Sweetbriar, we went down to the dining room for tea. Two of the ladies, one at each end of the long, exquisitely appointed table, presided over the tea and coffee services respectively. There were small silver salvers of thin, thin sandwiches wreathed in English cress, tiny biscuits with ham, and crisp sugar cookies. I usually made it a point to visit the bathroom on the ground floor where there was a magnificent throne that completely obscured the toilet. The Astors and their tea guests were never exposed to the vulgarity of uncovered plumbing fixtures, a kind of delicacy that I admired deeply, as I did the teas, which were an ultimate example of refinement.

Ah, the formal tea! How delectable, how utterly, Englishly upper class! The silver service, the pitchers for cream, the silver sugar bowls all set on silver trays. Who has time today for all that silver polishing? Certainly not I. But a tea is a charming way of entertaining, and it doesn't really have to include sterling silver. You will want a pot for tea and one for hot water (matching if possible), a tea strainer, attractive cups and saucers, a sugar bowl, a cream pitcher, silver spoons, and a dish for sliced lemon. In addition to sugar (preferably multicolored rock crystal), you will want to offer artificial sweetener. Sandwiches of cucumbers, watercress, cream cheese and jelly, and salmon should be passed, as well as biscuits and preserves and small cakes. Sometimes I add a bowl of strawberries with stems on, and slices of pound or raisin cake.

A variation of the above is the English high tea which we adapt to American customs occasionally on a late Sunday afternoon. We may offer an expanded tea menu, including somewhat more substantial sandwiches, scones, preserves, berries with clotted cream, and cake, all of which our guests tell us is "loverly"; and a five-thirty or six o'clock tea allows them to be home in time for their favorite television programs.

All this said, there are no hard and fast rules about when or what to serve at any time. One of our most delightful friends has a highly developed sweet tooth and is inclined to give dessert buffets at such odd hours as four or five o'clock on a weekend afternoon. She scours the city for specialties from various bakery shops and presents her guests with a choice of chocolate mousses, mocha tortes, coconut layer cakes, fruit pies, pecan rolls, and lemon roulades. Glasses of champagne are available to wash everything down. It's a high-calorie binge, and cholesterol be damned, but my! it's delicious to sin a bit every now and then. Actually, this type of buffet takes the place of supper, since no one can possibly face food again for at least fifteen hours.

Six to Nine in the Evening

I am not fond of cocktail parties, except as fund raisers for political candidates, but they do enable busy people to see a large number of friends and acquaintances at one time, and it is easier to invite someone we know slightly, but whom we would like to entertain, to a cocktail party than to a smaller and more intimate dinner. Still, I have never felt that cocktail parties fit under the heading of "hospitality." Nonetheless, they are convenient for "killing people off," and when we are indebted to a number of people, this is an advantage.

There are times when large cocktail parties are appropriate, and on those occasions both of us make an extra effort to circulate and to talk to as many guests as possible in the course of the rather brief time they will be in our home. We make sure that the bar is readily accessible and, if the party is really large, that there are several bars so that guests will not wait interminably for drinks. And we ensure that there will be a constantly circulating supply of hot and cold hors d'oeuvres, so that guests who are not planning to go on for dinner afterward will have enough food to sustain them through the night. When we go to a cocktail party, Randy is liable to say to me, "Do I fill up here or will we go to a restaurant afterward?"

Of course, an early-evening event need not be a cocktail party. Supper on a Sunday night gives people for whom the day has seemed endless something to look forward to. The menu can be a single-dish casserole of meat and vegetables that has been languishing in the freezer, and a store-bought fruit pie. Whatever we serve, we make sure that its preparation doesn't use the time necessary to complete reading the Sunday papers, and that the consumption of the meal does not keep our guests from returning to their own homes by eight o'clock, if they choose.

Ten-thirty to Midnight

My mother-in-law used to give formal seated suppers after stadium concerts in summer. The food was light, of the creamed chicken and rice variety, but the guests were heavy. I remember Mayor La

Guardia humming arias from *La Bohème* and Paul Robeson balanced precariously on a small gilt chair. And Mrs. Drum, wife of the commanding general of Governor's Island in the New York Bay, who, between mouthfuls of chicken, explained that the army had been wonderful "before this war, but now they're letting everybody in." General Drum was a regular at these late soirees, because he was able to get as much gasoline as he needed, and so he was allowed to drive us to the concerts. There are many reasons for entertaining that have little to do with friendship.

And if breakfast, or brunch, or even tea isn't *your* cup of tea, there is always the dinner party or the buffet supper, given with so much charm, originality, and éclat that you will have hoards of enthusiastic guests clamoring to reciprocate, and you will never have time to entertain again.

16

Weekend Guests

Hospitality from Friday to Sunday

The weekend guests have come to stay
They brought a lovely hors d'oeuvres tray
Of which we have a dozen more
From weekend guests who came before
Who think that we are constant servers
Of nothing else but cold hors d'oeuvers
But still we're happy that they came
And hoping that they feel the same
For guests of ours can do no wrong
Unless of course they stay too long.

When the nest has been emptied, there is apt to be an extra room available for conversion to a den or a library. If you are the type who enjoys extended entertaining you will probably do without the den and choose, instead, to use the space as a guest room. (Be wary of the returning fledgling who may decide to settle in if not discouraged.)

One-meal entertainment makes it possible to keep in touch with friends. Weekend visits enable you to develop closer relationships with people you care about, and whom you may see too rarely. At times, however, an extended period of togetherness may have the opposite effect. We have spent both lovely and awful weekends at the homes of our friends; and we have entertained guests who were sensitive, as well as enduring some who were philistines. Certain ground rules and considerations must be observed on both sides in order for a weekend visit to go smoothly.

Randy and I remember the dubious pleasures of sweltering through an August weekend in a room with no air conditioning and one attic-size window; getting dressed in a room with no mirror except a framed and cracked antique in which it was impossible to see anything (obviously purchased at a flea market by our hostess, who frequented such hunting grounds); huddling in a bed with no extra blankets when the temperature plunged in the middle of the night; trying to unpack and finding all available drawer space filled with the host's winter sweaters; and wondering how to hang three skirts and two pairs of trousers on two wire hangers. Not all of the above made life less than bearable in any one guest room at any one time, but a single one was enough to make home seem sweet.

On the other hand, as hosts, we have managed to survive weekend guests who expected extraordinary service. During the course of one memorable weekend we had a lady guest who suffered from an unquenchable thirst. She was, in fact, unendingly and demandingly thirsty. At ten-minute intervals she called plaintive attention to this fact and sat waiting while Randy or I ran to get water, iced tea, lemonade, or gin and tonic. It happened to be a weekend when we were having a large dinner party, and we had only recently moved into a newly finished house. All the chores we had counted on doing went undone, as were we by the end of the weekend.

Friends of ours had a similar experience with a couple whom they knew rather slightly, but whom they had foolishly invited to visit them in their very simple cabin in the woods. There were no servants to pass drinks or carry luggage, but our friends assumed their guests would enjoy the informality of a quiet, unscheduled weekend. They should have been warned when the couple arrived with sufficient luggage for a month's stay and watched politely as the host struggled upstairs with three heavy bags. The final straw, however, was not placed on the camel's back until Saturday night, when the host discovered the guests' shoes placed outside the guest-room door, obviously waiting to be polished and returned before morning. After some discussion with his wife, he carefully filled the shoes with flowers and went to bed.

As our new house became older and more settled, we became wiser. We no longer catered to unreasonable demands that spoiled weekends for us, but we also learned how to make guests comfortable. To accomplish this we made lists of items that should be in a well-accoutered guest room, and we checked periodically in order to ensure that everything was where it should be.

We heard about the value of lists from a friend who had just moved into a new home. Having spent weekends with various friends during the preceding years, she had assembled a record of what should be available in a guest bathroom. Satisfied with the results of her research, she put out towels and washcloths and arranged the appropriate pharmaceutical supplies in the bathroom: perfume, cosmetics, toothbrushes, aspirin and Tylenol, and mouthwash. She taped the list to the medicine-cabinet door, kissed her guests good night, and went happily to bed, having quite forgotten to put out any toilet paper, thus proving that even carefully prepared lists need constant reviewing.

The following is our "how to keep hosts and guests happy over a weekend" list. It contains nothing that is unfamiliar to frequent hosts, but the most frequent are the most likely to become complacent and forgetful:

1.   Difficult friends should be invited for dinner, but never overnight.

2. Guests should be informed, well in advance, of all the plans for the weekend and exactly what clothing they will need. They may not enjoy being stuffed into a too-small borrowed bathing suit because no one told them that lunch would be served on floating trays in the middle of the pool. Clear instructions not only prevent the ruinous borrowing and stretching of your new bathing suit, but also may save your more cautious guests from developing backaches caused by carrying suitcases loaded with their entire wardrobes.

3. The weekend plans should allow for rest as well as recreation. Filling every minute is not kind or considerate. A good weekend doesn't mean Sunday-night collapse. You may be able to rest on Monday, your guests may not. On Friday night you may want to give a small dinner, and on Saturday night perhaps friends who live nearby will entertain. If there is to be tennis or golf or skiing, or any other planned activity during the days, do allow plenty of time for rest before the evening festivities. We had guests from Minnesota visit us in New York a few years ago. I planned sightseeing all day and theater at night. On the third day my friends said firmly, "We don't want to see another museum, or the top of another building, ever! We're going shopping and we'll be back later this afternoon." Guests have a right to a voice, and a choice, in at least some of the activities.

4. Hosts should sleep in their own guest rooms at least once every other month, or at least go through some sort of dry run in advance of any weekend on which they expect guests. The last couple may have walked off with half the medicine-cabinet supplies. It is amazing to discover how uncomfortable a well-planned guest room can become if it is neglected for any extended period of time.

5. Plan simple meals that can be cooked in advance and stored in the freezer, so that you won't spend your entire weekend in the kitchen. Breakfast can be a help-yourself affair, with orange juice in a pitcher, coffee maker ready to be plugged in, bread ready to be popped into the toaster, jam and marmalade in small pots, and boxes of cold cereal set out on the counter. The night before you

will have given the guests careful instructions about finding milk, orange juice, and butter or margarine in the refrigerator, in case you outsleep them. Lunch should be just as simple: a hearty salad, fruit, and cookies. Unless you have help, dinner for more than four or six should be served buffet-style.

6.   The following items should be checked regularly, before the guests arrive:

- Are there hangers for skirts and pants? Are there enough to accommodate guests who, in spite of your thorough instructions, came with clothing for every event and every change in temperature?

- Have you cleared the closet and at least two bureau drawers of your possessions?

- Is there a small television set? An inexpensive black-and-white set will do. Today, television is available in motel rooms, and your guest room should be competitive with, or better than, the average Holiday Inn.

- Is there a small bowl of fruit so that if dinner is late the guests can nibble a bit to assuage hunger?

- Does the medicine cabinet have some of the supplies that guests may have forgotten to bring: aspirin and Tylenol, or one of the other analgesics; toilet water; bath powder; bobby pins; mouthwash, toothbrush, and toothpaste; deodorant; hairspray?

- Are the basic supplies in place? You should provide your guests with bath towels, wash cloths, hand or face towels, extra blankets, soap, a shower cap, a small sewing kit purloined from a stay in a hotel or motel, and, of course, toilet paper, with an extra roll. Incidentally, it is worthwhile observing the bathroom supplies provided in good hotels and motels. They have been chosen by experts and can help you prepare your own list.

- Is it comfortable, or even possible, for the guests to read in bed? This means that lights should be directed so that one person can read while the other sleeps. The lights should be easy to turn off without having to get out of bed, and bright enough so that paperback print is legible. A small selection of books (frequently updated) on a table near a chair with a reading lamp is a nice touch. Short stories, short detective and mystery novels, and a magazine or two are best, but be sure to throw out last year's *Newsweek* or *Time*. Also avoid a six-hundred-page novel; it might induce the guests to stay over for the week or to walk off with the book.

7.   This may be the most important item on the list: Make your guests feel wanted and as much like members of your family as possible. Be delighted to see them arrive and control your delight at their departure.

L'Envoi

*The party's done, the guests have fled
Good night, sweet Prince, and so to bed!*

It is pleasant to receive word that our guests enjoyed the food; found their fellow guests amusing; and, in the case of weekenders, found the beds comfortable; and think well of us as hosts. All this can be conveyed in a brief note; no one wants to receive, and have to read, four pages of hyperbole. A statement that "you are the greatest!" is quite sufficient. Of course the most convincing testimony of appreciation is neither a bouquet, an hors d'oeuvre tray, nor a note, although these are pleasant to receive, but the fact that within a reasonable time all of our guests, including even the single gentlemen, will request "the pleasure of *our* company."

Acknowledgments

Thanks to my new friends at Clarkson N. Potter, with deep appreciation for their wisdom and advice: Nancy Kahan, Pam Krauss, Carol Southern, and Martha Schueneman. And of course to the friends we have entertained and who have entertained us, with gratitude for their tolerance and for sharing their "fallen soufflé" anecdotes with me.